Robert J. Kus, RN, PhD
Editor

Addiction and Recovery in Gay and Lesbian Persons

Pre-Publication
REVIEWS,
COMMENTARIES,
EVALUATIONS . . .

A *ddiction and Recovery in Gay and Lesbian Persons* is a significant guide for both gay and heterosexual providers, offering a wealth of insights into the treatment and care of gay and lesbian clients in recovery from chemical dependency.

This book has helpful sections on dysfunctional patterns in relationships, and the prevention of relapse in HIV positive clients. It outlines the social context of internalized homophobia, challenges homophobic messages in religious addiction, and affirms gay-positive spirituality. *Addiction and Recovery* is a vital resource for anyone providing services for gay, lesbian, and bisexual clients.

Rik Isensee, LCSW
Author, LOVE BETWEEN MEN, and GROWING UP GAY IN A DYSFUNCTIONAL FAMILY

"**A**ddiction and Recovery in Gay and Lesbian Persons" is an excellent collection of multi-faceted articles pertaining to life-style needs and problems when alcohol/chemical use becomes abuse or addiction. Will chemical dependency treatment be successful if the true sexuality of s-he remains hidden or denied? Could this be me? Could this be you? Could our needs be ignored or not addressed because the staff is not properly trained or aware of competent referral resources?

The editor and contributors have tackled a poorly understood societal problem and have produced an enlightening book that is *very readable and useful* for therapists, counselors, health professionals, clergy, etc. But, as important, it can, and will, hopefully BE READ BY ALL AMERICANS. These authors have "told it like it is" in an easy non-confrontive and informative manner that should provoke healthy discussion and thought about this underserved population.

Some of the subjects include: codependency, chemical dependency, sexual attitudes, sexuality, healthy friendships and relationships, and importantly, self-worth.

With increasing heavy chemical use comes increasing denial and deception. This dishonesty often becomes a double whammy if that person is gay or lesbian–trying to hide both the addiction and the sexuality from employers, family, friends and often themselves. CD treatment centers, support groups, families and society are often as hungup on sexual issues as the client obtaining treatment. Particularly in rural America, I see repeated alcoholism/chemical relapses which appear to be tied to not dealing with bisexuality/homosexuality and often internalized homophobia. Books likes this one help alleviate future tragedies as we all learn to extend our helping hands.

In reading this book you may see characteristics of peers, friends, family or yourself, and in so doing, open your mind to learning about many suffering people. This book may be placed in a brown paper bag and hidden under a pile of clothes in the back closet but it belongs in our hands or on the bookshelf to remind ourselves and others that there are still serious problems to be addressed and resolved.

Herbert R. Hedge, D.D.S.
Director, Dental Alcohol Consulting Services, Adjunct Assistant Professor College of Dentistry, University of Iowa, Iowa City, Iowa

Addiction and Recovery in Gay and Lesbian Persons

Addiction and Recovery in Gay and Lesbian Persons

Robert J. Kus, RN, PhD
Editor

Addiction and Recovery in Gay and Lesbian Persons, edited by Robert J. Kus, was simultaneously issued by The Haworth Press, Inc., under the same title, as a special issue of the *Journal of Gay & Lesbian Social Services*, Volume 2, Number 1, 1995, James J. Kelly, and Raymond M. Berger, Editors.

Harrington Park Press
An Imprint of
The Haworth Press, Inc.
New York · London

1-56023-055-X

Published by

Harrington Park Press, 10 Alice Street, Binghamton, NY 13904-1580 USA

Harrington Park Press is an imprint of the Haworth Press, Inc., 10 Alice Street, Bing-hamton, NY 13904-1580 USA.

Addiction and Recovery in Gay and Lesbian Persons has also been published as *Journal of Gay & Lesbian Social Services,* Volume 2, Number 1 1995.

The development, preparation, and publication of this work has been undertaken with great care. However, the publisher, employees, editors, and agents of The Haworth Press and all imprints of The Haworth Press, Inc., including The Haworth Medical Press and Pharmaceutical Products Press, are not responsible for any errors contained herein or for consequences that may ensue from use of materials or information contained in this work. Opinions expressed by the author(s) are not neces-sarily those of The Haworth Press, Inc.

The Haworth Press, Inc., 10 Alice Street, Binghamton, NY 13904-1580 USA

Library of Congress Cataloging-in-Publication Data

Addiction and recovery in gay and lesbian persons / Robert J. Kus, editor.
          p. cm.
          ". . . also been published as Journal of gay & lesbian social services, volume 2, number 1, 1995"–T.p. verso.
          Includes bibliographical references and index.
          ISBN 1-56024-668-5 (thp : acid free paper). -- ISBN 1-56023-055-X (hpp : acid free paper)
          1. Lesbians--United States--Alcohol use. 2. Lesbians--United States--Drug use. 3. Gay men--United States--Alcohol use. 4. Gay men--United States--Drug use. 5. Alcoholics--Rehabilitation-United States. 6. Narcotic addicts--Rehabilitation--United States.
I. Kus, Robert J.
HV5139.A33   1995
362.29'2'08664--dc20   95-1683
                                                                                                 CIP

To my friend Jim in the Big Sky Country.

INDEXING & ABSTRACTING

Contributions to this publication are selectively indexed or abstracted in print, electronic, online, or CD-ROM version(s) of the reference tools and information services listed below. This list is current as of the copyright date of this publication. See the end of this section for additional notes.

- *AIDS Newsletter (CAB Abstracts)*, CAB International, Wallingford Oxon OX10 8DE, England

- *Cambridge Scientific Abstracts, Risk Abstracts,* Cambridge Information Group, 7200 Wisconsin Avenue #601, Bethesda, MD 20814

- *caredata CD: the social and community care database,* National Institute for Social Work, 5 Tavistock Place, London WC1H 9SS, England

- *Digest of Neurology and Psychiatry,* The Institute of Living, 400 Washington Street, Hartford, CT 06106

- *ERIC Clearinghouse on Urban Education (ERIC/CUE),* Teachers College, Columbia University, Box 40, New York, NY 10027

- *Family Life Educator "Abstracts Section,"* ETR Associates, P.O. Box 1830, Santa Cruz, CA 95061-1830

- *Index to Periodical Articles Related to Law,* University of Texas, 727 East 26th Street, Austin, TX 78705

- *Inventory of Marriage and Family Literature (online and hard copy),* National Council on Family Relations, 3989 Central Avenue NE, Suite 550, Minneapolis, MN 55421

- *Referativnyi Zhurnal (Abstracts Journal of the Institute of Scientific Information of the Republic of Russia),* The Institute of Scientific Information, Baltijskaja ul., 14, Moscow A-219, Republic of Russia

- *Social Work Abstracts,* National Association of Social Workers, 750 First Street NW, 8th Floor, Washington, DC 20002

(continued)

- *Sociological Abstracts (SA),* Sociological Abstracts, Inc., P.O. Box 22206, San Diego, CA 92192-0206

- *Studies on Women Abstracts,* Carfax Publishing Company, P.O. Box 25, Abingdon, Oxfordshire OX14 3UE, United Kingdom

- *Violence and Abuse Abstracts: A Review of Current Literature on Interpersonal Violence (VAA),* Sage Publications, Inc., 2455 Teller Road, Newbury Park, CA 91320

SPECIAL BIBLIOGRAPHIC NOTES

*related to special journal issues (separates)
and indexing/abstracting*

☐ indexing/abstracting services in this list will also cover material in any "separate" that is co-published simultaneously with Haworth's special thematic journal issue or DocuSerial. Indexing/abstracting usually covers material at the article/chapter level.

☐ monographic co-editions are intended for either non-subscribers or libraries which intend to purchase a second copy for their circulating collections.

☐ monographic co-editions are reported to all jobbers/wholesalers/approval plans. The source journal is listed as the "series" to assist the prevention of duplicate purchasing in the same manner utilized for books-in-series.

☐ to facilitate user/access services all indexing/abstracting services are encouraged to utilize the co-indexing entry note indicated at the bottom of the first page of each article/chapter/contribution.

☐ this is intended to assist a library user of any reference tool (whether print, electronic, online, or CD-ROM) to locate the monographic version if the library has purchased this version but not a subscription to the source journal.

☐ individual articles/chapters in any Haworth publication are also available through the Haworth Document Delivery Services (HDDS).

CONTENTS

ABOUT THE EDITOR

Robert J. Kus, RN, PhD, a nurse-sociologist, specializes in gay men's studies and alcohol studies. In addition to studying sobriety in gay American men, he has been conducting cross-cultural gay men's studies in Europe where he has presented over 25 workshops and papers. The author of almost 30 book chapters and journal articles, Dr. Kus is also the editor of *Keys to Caring: Assisting Your Gay and Lesbian Clients* (Alyson, 1990), *Gay Men of Alcoholics Anonymous: First-Hand Accounts* (WinterStar Press, 1990), and *Spirituality and Chemical Dependency* (The Haworth Press, Inc., in press). He is currently practicing nursing at Laurelwood Hospital in Willoughby, Ohio, and is studying to become a Roman Catholic priest.

ABOUT THE CONTRIBUTORS

Ethan E. Bickelhaupt, MD, FAPA, is a physician who specializes in family practice, psychiatry, and addiction medicine in Perry and Topeka, Kansas. Dr. Bickelhaupt received his BS in zoology from The College of Idaho and his MD from the University of Washington School of Medicine in Seattle. Dr. Bickelhaupt is a Diplomat of the American Board of Psychiatry and Neurology in both general and geriatric psychiatry. He is certified by the American Society of Addiction Medicine and is a Fellow of the American Psychiatric Association. Ethan has a long history of service to the gay and lesbian communities dating back to his medical school days in Seattle, service which includes writing, speaking, teaching, and counseling. Currently, Dr. Bickelhaupt, in addition to his varied practice, serves as Medical Director of the Senior Diagnostic and Treatment Unit at the Stormont-Vail Medical Center and as a Consultant to the Chemical Dependency Unit at the St. Francis Hospital and Medical Center in Topeka, Kansas.

LeClair Bissell, MD, is an author, researcher and lecturer living in Sanibel, Florida. She received her bachelor's degree from the University of Colorado and her master's degree in library science and an MD at Columbia University in New York City. She specializes in alcoholism and other drug dependencies in special populations. She is co-author of *The cat who drank too much* (Bibulophile Press, 1982), *Alcoholism in the professions* (Oxford University Press, 1984), *Ethics for addiction professionals* (Hazelden, 1987), *Chemical dependency in nursing* (Addison-Wesley, 1989), and *To care enough: Intervention with chemically dependent colleagues* (Johnson Institute, 1989), as well as many scientific papers, pamphlets and book chapters. Recent publications include stories of alcoholic pharmacists, women physicians, and doctoral level psychologists and of co-dependency in physicians, nurses and alcoholism counselors. Dr. Bissell is currently studying veterinarians, men nurses, and both gay and lesbian professionals in many disciplines. She is also active as an AIDS educator and is a hotline volunteer for the Lee County Task Force.

Fr. Leo Booth, MTh, CAC, CEDC, is a nationally acclaimed author, educator and trainer on spirituality and recovery from depression, addictions, and low self-esteem. A recovering alcoholic, he is an Episcopal priest as well as a certified addictions and eating disorders counselor. Born in England, he was raised in a religiously divided home, which contributed to his alcoholism and later, to his focus on unhealthy religious messages as a source of depression and low self-esteem. He has developed a unique new spirituality model based on a healthy relationship between body, mind, and emotions. He presents workshops, lectures and inservice trainings to therapists, associations, hospitals and treatment programs nationwide. His latest book is *When God becomes a drug: Breaking the chains of religious addiction and abuse.* Father Leo is Parish Priest of St. George's Episcopal Church, Hawthorne, California, outside Los Angeles. For further information or a catalog of Father Leo's books and tapes, call Spiritual Concepts, (310)-434-4813.

Dana G. Finnegan, PhD, CAC, is the Co-Founder and Co-Director of Discovery Counseling Center, an agency specializing in services to women, lesbians, gay men, and those affected by alcoholism and drug abuse and sexual identity problems. Dr. Finnegan has done extensive service for gay and lesbian persons. She is the Co-Founder of the National Association of Lesbian and Gay Alcoholism Professionals (NALGAP), co-author of many gay/lesbian journal articles, book chapters, and bibliographies, and a frequent speaker at national conferences. Dr. Finnegan is co-author (with Emily McNally) of *Dual identities: Counseling chemically dependent gay men and lesbians* (Hazelden, 1987) and (with T. McGinnis) is co-author of *Open family and marriage: A guide to personal growth* (C. V. Mosby, 1976). She is Senior Editor of the *Journal of Chemical Dependency Treatment* and a member of the editorial board of *Alcoholism Treatment Quarterly.* In the summer months, Dr. Finnegan teaches at the Rutgers University Summer School of Alcohol Studies.

Cheryl Hetherington, PhD, Founder of Hetherington & Associates in Iowa City, Iowa, is a psychologist, training consultant and writer in private practice. She is an adjunct faculty member at The University of Iowa in Counselor Education and a residency supervisor in the Department of Psychiatry. Dr. Hetherington received her PhD from The Pennsylvania State University in counselor education. She has been a therapist, faculty member and administrator at several colleges since 1972. Presently Dr. Hetherington is a therapist specializing in women's concerns, recovery issues, and life transitions. She has presented hundreds of wellness and stress management programs using a light-hearted, practical approach. Dr. Hetherington is the author of two books: *Bringing your self to life: Changing co-dependent patterns* (Rudi, 1990) and *Working with groups from dysfunctional families: Structured exercises to promote health* (Whole Person Press, 1992).

Sheppard B. Kominars, PhD, is a prolific author, playwright, and lecturer. Dr. Kominars received his BA from Kenyon College, an MA from Columbia University, and his PhD from Boston University. Over the past dozen years, he has specialized in recovery issues in gay and lesbian persons and presented workshops and seminars in these issues all over the United States for helping professionals. He is the author of *Accepting ourselves: The Twelve Step journey of recovery from addiction in gay men and lesbians* (Harper Collins, 1987) which has sold over 20,000 copies. Dr. Kominars has been an active member of both the Pennsylvania and California Diocesan Commissions on Alcoholism and Substance Abuse. He is a playwright and Chairman of the Board of the Playwrights' Center of San Francisco. Sheppard has three children and now lives with his partner, Marv, and their two Burmese kittens, Patience and Serenity.

Robert J. Kus, RN, PhD, is a nurse-sociologist who specializes in gay men's studies and alcohol studies. He has a BA in sociology from Cleveland State University, an MS in psychiatric-mental health nursing from the University of Oklahoma, and a PhD in sociology from the University of Montana. In addition to studying sobriety in gay American men, Dr. Kus has been conducting cross-cultural gay men's studies in Europe where he has presented over

25 workshops and papers. In addition to more than 30 book chapters and journal articles which have been published, Dr. Kus has edited *Gay men of Alcoholics Anonymous: First-hand accounts* (WinterStar Press, 1990), *Keys to caring: Assisting your gay and lesbian clients* (Alyson, 1990), and *Spirituality and chemical dependency* (The Haworth Press, Inc., in press). After teaching for ten years at The University of Iowa, Bob moved to Ohio in 1992 where he is currently studying for the Catholic priesthood.

Rev. Mark A. Latcovich, MDiv, MA, is a Roman Catholic priest of the Diocese of Cleveland and Assistant Professor of systematics and pastoral theology at St. Mary Seminary, Wickliffe, Ohio. He is currently working on a PhD in Sociology at Case Western Reserve University in Cleveland and has participated in the Institute of Social Research at the University of Michigan in Ann Arbor. His specialties include the sociology of religion, family, and aging.

Emily B. McNally, PhD, CAC, is a certified alcoholism counselor and licensed psychologist. Dr. McNally is Co-Founder and Co-Director of Discovery Counseling Center in Millburn, NJ and New York City. Emily is Co-Founder of the National Association of Lesbian and Gay Alcoholism Professionals (NALGAP) and has taught in the Rutgers University Summer School of Alcohol Studies. In addition to her journal articles and professional presentations, Dr. McNally has co-authored (with Dana Finnegan) *Dual identities: Counseling chemically dependent gay men and lesbians* (Hazelden, 1987). In her 1989 doctoral dissertation done at New York University, Dr. McNally developed a stage model of identity transformation in lesbian recovering alcoholics in Alcoholics Anonymous. She makes her home in Greenwich Village.

Melvin I. Pohl, MD, is a Family Practitioner and Clinical Director of Addiction Services, Montevista Hospital, Las Vegas, Nevada. He is also Medical Director of Substance Abuse Services, Behavioral Healthcare Options, Las Vegas. Certified by the American Society of Addiction Medicine (ASAM), Dr. Pohl co-chaired three of ASAM's National Forums on AIDS and Chemical Dependency. He is Chairman of ASAM's AIDS Committee and a Fellow of the American

Academy of Family Practice. He has published numerous works on AIDS and addictions and is a nationally known public speaker. Dr. Pohl is co-author of *The caregivers' journey: When you love someone with AIDS* (Harper/Hazelden, 1990). His new book was released in 1993 by Health Communications and is entitled *Staying sane: When you care for someone with chronic illness.*

George Byron Smith, MSN, RN, is Director of Adult Comprehensive Services at Tampa General Hospital-University Psychiatry Center. Mr. Smith received both his undergraduate and graduate degrees in nursing from The University of Texas Medical Branch in Galveston, Texas. He specializes in psychiatric and chemical dependency nursing and nursing management. He was honored by the American Psychiatric Nurses' Association Smoyak Writing Award in 1992 for his writing in psychiatric nursing. George's research and publications focus on gay and lesbian issues, and he is a member of the Editorial Board of the *Journal of Psychosocial Nursing and Mental Health Services.* George serves on the Board of Directors of the AIDS Coalition of Pinellas, an organization serving HIV/AIDS clients in the Tampa Bay area. George makes his home on the Florida west coast in Tampa with his life-partner Roger, their two pugs Geoffy and Gus, and their Boston terrier Grover.

Foreword

Battles over the civil rights of gay and lesbian people are increasing in number and intensity as the 1990s draw rapidly to an end. Amid almost daily reports of new victories or setbacks, the only certainty is change. This American civic conflict is finding expression in every one of our major social institutions.

Before his election, President Bill Clinton promised to lift the ban on gays and lesbians in the military and included openly gay people among both his campaign and transitional staff. Vice President Dan Quayle crusaded for "traditional family values," somehow ignoring that most gay people grew up in such families, while Republican candidate Pat Buchanan made clear that he finds homosexuality a litmus test for moral impurity. Initiatives appeared on the ballots in Oregon and Colorado to deny gays and lesbians the protection of civil rights laws. In Oregon the initiative was voted down. In Colorado it succeeded, which provoked a series of boycotts by organizations that had planned to meet in that state.

In many mainstream churches, gays are welcomed as congregants, if not with wild enthusiasm, at least with politeness and a degree of warmth. In others, they are now formally included as clergy as well. Some denominations now recognize same-sex committed relationships, either by performing a marriage or through similar ceremonies under a different name. Reform Judaism formalizes gay relationships while Orthodox do not. The Rev. Jerry Falwell and Rev. Pat Robertson have joined New York's Cardinal O'Connor in urging ordinarily decent people to act upon their fears and anxieties rather than on their virtues. Journalist Peter Gomes

[Haworth co-indexing entry note]: "Foreword." Bissell, LeClair. Co-published simultaneously in *Journal of Gay & Lesbian Social Services* (The Haworth Press, Inc.) Vol. 2, No. 1, 1995, pp. xxi-xxv: and: *Addiction and Recovery in Gay and Lesbian Persons* (ed: Robert J. Kus) The Haworth Press, Inc., 1995, pp. xix-xxiii. Multiple copies of this article/chapter may be purchased from The Haworth Document Delivery Center [1-800-3-HAWORTH; 9:00 a.m. - 5:00 p.m. (EST)].

writes in the *New York Times* that hatred of homosexuality is the last respectable prejudice of the century.

In the arts, it is now possible to present plays and movie scripts in which gay and lesbian characters do not die conveniently at the end of the story. Some are even allowed happy endings. Although major sponsors of TV shows still often bow to the urging of the organized religious right to avoid showing gays and lesbians at all or to present them as amusing stereotypes, we now and then see a few as simply ordinary people. The famous lesbian kiss shown on L.A. Law was followed by the disappearance of the lesbian character from the series. The National Endowment for the Arts has been under fire and its funding threatened ever since it dared exhibit the photographs of gay artist Robert Mapplethorpe. On the other hand, the almost total silence of the 30s and 40s about gays and lesbians and the obligatory suicide in the final chapter of the 50s novels have been replaced by dozens of excellent books. Rita Mae Brown, Paul Monette, Alice Walker, Audre Lorde and many others now speak freely to a wide audience and are no longer limited to a handful of small independent gay and lesbian publications.

Scientists are seriously debating whether or not sexual orientation is genetic. There is increasing evidence that it may well be. Some react to this notion with anger. "You're trying to get them off the hook!" Some gays respond with relief, "There, you see! It's not our fault. We were born different." I find myself interested in the findings and in the discussions, even intrigued. It's gratifying to see a puzzle being solved and to understand something better, but I am put off by both sides when the issue is couched in terms of blame. Unless one believes there is something basically wrong or undesirable about a given sexual orientation, the question of blame shouldn't be part of the discussion. Difference, yes. Guilt or innocence, no.

How to write about the gay community in the 90s without talking about AIDS? Soon all of us will know someone who is HIV+ or will lose a friend or family member. Those of us who work with addicts and/or are part of the gay and lesbian communities had that experience early. Some of us have lost as many as forty friends and acquaintances. The grieving never ends. Loss follows loss. Friends, patients, casual acquaintances are rumored to be sick. Then they are sick. Many of them die. More and more are living with AIDS in our fears, in ourselves, in our community. For example, in the American Society of Addiction Medicine, a relatively small organization of some 3,500 physicians of which I'm a member, I know of five colleagues whom we have lost. There are probably others. At least two have lost children to the epidemic. Grief is and will continue to be something to address in working with gay and lesbian people, grief and the anger that go with watching long years of denial and neglect from an administration in Washington that permitted talk of "innocent victims of AIDS" and reserved its compassion only for transfusion recipients and small (presumably asexual?) children.

People, when drunk, are by definition incapable of sober judgement. Craving for drugs and the urging of getting the next pipe or next injection make concerns about clean needles or safer sex easy to forget. Young people who have been well taught about the risks admit freely that, after a few beers, they can't always be bothered with condoms. Drugs, alcohol and HIV go hand in hand. All alcoholics and addicts can be considered to be at risk for AIDS if they have a history of any sexually transmitted disease and are sexually active. Although they are not always aware of the fact, those who work in the chemical dependency field are routinely treating people with HIV, many of them gay or lesbian.

As the numbers of infected people continue to rise, we can expect to see more backlash against people who are or are thought to be infected. There are increasing reports of gay bashings, with both men and women under attack. For historical reasons too familiar to need repeating here, gay men and their lifestyles are still seen by many as causing the epidemic and now threatening the larger society. True or not, rational or not, the fear is real. We are increasingly a violent society, prone to settle differences with guns and fists. When even the law excludes gays and lesbians from basic civil rights protections, small wonder that thugs take up their baseball bats for an evening's amusement, attacking gays.

What about AA? The International Advisory Council that prints a directory of gay and lesbian AA groups lists over 800 regular meetings in the United States. There are probably many more unknown to them. Some of those they list only once actually have many meetings per week. For example, one meets five times a day, seven days a week. There are five groups listed in Australia, forty-five in Canada, fifteen in Germany, and individual meetings in such diverse places as South Africa and Oman. This is certainly a far cry from the days spent by Dr. Bob's Akron group debating whether or not a man with "another problem" could be admitted to AA! (The decision in his favor led to the AA tradition that the only requirement for membership is a desire to stop drinking.) Many major cities like New Orleans and Chicago have gay 12-step club houses, and there are many weekend roundups for gay and lesbian members which are listed in the calendar section of the *AA Grapevine*. Many regular AA groups are comfortable with openly gay and lesbian members, while others are not. In so far as AA reflects society as a whole, its members are subject to most of the same prejudices and fears that others have. For that reason, it behooves a therapist to know the attitudes of groups and individuals before urging a new gay or lesbian alcoholic or addict to attend and tell all.

Do gay and lesbian people have more addiction problems than others? This has not been easy data to get and some that has been published to date is none too reliable. I think it is fair to say that many gays and lesbians leave smaller communities for cities to find wider social opportunities. The major gay and lesbian urban social groups do find drinking quite acceptable. A newcomer will be introduced to the bars and given every opportunity to drink. For some, with exposure will come problems.

Many suggest that alcoholism and addiction are caused by stress. I do not believe it's that simple. I don't think that stress alone makes anyone alcoholic, though it certainly doesn't mitigate against it. Gays and lesbians in our culture are undeniably under stress. It is still risky for many even to come out to their own families. Jobs are lost, promotions denied, physical attacks happen. Friends may accept or shy away. There are endless decisions to be made about whether or not to come out to an individual or in a particular situation. Maybe the gay community has considerably more alcohol and drug exposure than the extended culture. I don't know. I'm sure it doesn't have less.

I am equally sure that gays and lesbians continue to have difficulty in finding good addiction treatment. Though it is less and less common, there are still instances of counselors who, when they discover that their clients are gay or lesbian, set about trying to change their orientation rather than treating their addiction. Patients have been assured that, once sober, they'll find themselves "normal." Others report that committed relationships of many years' duration still are ignored, while distant relatives are selected to participate in family treatment programs. Some patients fear going to a treatment facility where they may be ridiculed or rejected if they talk about the reality of their lives. There are similar fears about going to centers designed to treat gays and lesbians because of worries that if they are discovered there, their private lives become public knowledge.

One particularly bad episode concerned a man in residential treatment who was urged by his counselor to come out to a therapy group. He did. A few hours later, he was attacked by a group of fellow patients who threw a blanket over him so they could not be recognized, then beat him so badly he had to be hospitalized.

This collection of papers will contribute to what is a limited but rapidly growing body of knowledge about gays, lesbians, and chemical dependency. The literature remains small but we are learning. Once in the early 70s, I attended a meeting in the apartment of Ruth Fox, M.D., a pioneer in alcoholism treatment. Several physicians were chatting about their alcoholic patients, including one who stated flatly that all of his were schizophrenic. Another respected woman physician, not Dr. Fox, opined that many patients could recover anyway, except, of course, the homosexuals. She had never known one to recover. To my certain knowledge, there were three of them listening to these statements and carefully not making eye contact with each other. They did recover. They do recover. In the future, when gays and lesbians can be open and honest about their lives, they will recover more easily and in greater numbers.

LeClair Bissell, MD
Sanibel, Florida

Introduction

The Christophers and others have wisely held that, "It is better to light just one little candle than to curse the darkness." Likewise, it is much better to work to find solutions to life's problems than to go about complaining about the sorry state of affairs of the world. All of the contributors to this collection are candle-lighters, people committed to making the world a better place through their clinical practices, research, teaching, and/or writing in the area of gay and lesbian chemical dependency.

For the past fifteen years or so, there has been a growing awareness among gay and lesbian persons that chemical dependency is a major problem in their respective communities, a problem which denies humans freedom and dignity. How ironic to be destroyed by alcohol or other mind-altering drugs just when two great social movements–the Gay Liberation Movement and the Lesbian Feminist Movement–are seeking to offer gay and lesbian Americans freedom and pride!

Fortunately, helping professionals and scientists have become interested in how chemical dependency is affecting gay and lesbian persons and are offering some help. The purpose of this collection is to offer social workers and other interested persons a glimpse into some of the work being done in this field via presenting eight articles written by experts in the field. Needless to say, such a collection can only scratch the surface of the exciting things being done in this field. It is hoped that this collection will not only offer social workers some concrete information and ideas for treatment, but that it will whet their appetite for further exploration into the fascinating subspecialty of gay and lesbian chemical dependency.

[Haworth co-indexing entry note]: "Introduction." Kus, Robert J. Co-published simultaneously in *Journal of Gay & Lesbian Social Services* (The Haworth Press, Inc.) Vol. 2, No. 1, 1995, pp. 1-3; and: *Addiction and Recovery in Gay and Lesbian Persons* (ed: Robert J. Kus) The Haworth Press, Inc., 1995, pp. 1-3. Multiple copies of this article/chapter may be purchased from The Haworth Document Delivery Center [1-800-3-HAWORTH; 9:00 a.m. - 5:00 p.m. (EST)].

In the first article, "Alcoholism and drug abuse in gay and lesbian persons: A review of incidence studies," Dr. Ethan Bickelhaupt provides a synopsis of seven research studies which examined the incidence of chemical dependency in gay and/or lesbian persons. Six of the studies were done in the United States, and one was done in the Czech Republic. Each of the studies consistently shows a higher incidence of alcoholism and/or other forms of chemical dependency in gay and/or lesbian persons. Because this is the only article which gathers the information on gay/lesbian incidence studies in one place, it is destined to be a most treasured resource for researchers, clinicians, and others for some time.

In the second article, "Chemical dependency and HIV infection," Dr. Mel Pohl provides the reader with a basic, working knowledge of HIV infection and AIDS. Such information is critical for those who work with chemically dependent gay men in particular, as gay American men have been afflicted with AIDS more than any other social group in the United States. Dr. Pohl, an expert in both gay/lesbian chemical dependency and AIDS, also provides the reader with a helpful list of sexual activities in terms of their relative safety.

Dr. Sheppard Kominars explores the concept of homophobia in the third article. As he points out, homophobia, or the irrational hatred of gays, lesbians, and/or homosexuality, is a root problem which needs to be recognized and excised from society to lessen the internalized homophobia which serves to block recovery in gay and lesbian addicts. Dr. Sheppard, who has specialized in the field of gay and lesbian recovery issues for over a dozen years, provides concrete examples of homophobia in everyday life.

The fourth article, "Dysfunctional relationship patterns: Positive changes for gay and lesbian people," is contributed by Dr. Cheryl Hetherington, a psychologist who specializes in co-dependency and dysfunctional families. Dr. Hetherington provides the reader with the typical picture of the relationship problems which persons who grow up in dysfunctional families experience, for chemically dependent gay and lesbian couples experience the same difficulties.

In the fifth article, "Spirituality and the gay community," Fr. Leo Booth, an Episcopal priest who specializes in spirituality and recovery issues, talks about the difference between spirituality and religion and what are the special concerns of gay and lesbian persons. Because spirituality (via AA and other 12-Step groups) is the primary form of chemical dependency treatment in the United States, Fr. Booth's insights are very important for the helping professional to grasp.

The sixth article, "Special interest groups in Alcoholics Anonymous: A focus on gay men's groups," is contributed by Fr. Mark Latcovich and myself. In this work, we explore the concept of the "special interest group" in AA, especially as it applies to gay men. Because the 12-Step way of life is used by so many gay and lesbian alcoholics and addicts for their recovery, and because so many of them feel a need for gay-specific or lesbian-specific 12-Step groups for their recovery programs to be ideal, it is worthwhile exploring such groups in terms of their history, positive aspects, and limitations.

In the seventh article, "The National Association of Lesbian and Gay Alcoholism Professionals (NALGAP): A retrospective," NALGAP co-founders Dr. Dana Finnegan and Dr. Emily McNally talk about the organization in terms of why it was formed initially, the ups and downs it has experienced over the years, what it has accomplished, and what it needs to do for the future. While the NALGAP story is interesting in itself, I find Dana and Emily's candle-lighting efforts very inspirational: they saw an unmet need and they met it.

Finally, Mr. George Byron Smith and I provide social workers with ideas about referrals and resources in "Referrals and resources for chemically dependent gay and lesbian clients." In this article, we identify some of the special problems chemically dependent gay and lesbian clients may have, what kind of resources are available for help, and how to go about finding out where these resources are. Special consideration is given to the social worker in rural areas of America where gay and/or lesbian services are not readily visible or available.

Robert J. Kus, RN, PhD
Wickliffe, Ohio

Alcoholism and Drug Abuse
in Gay and Lesbian Persons:
A Review of Incidence Studies

Ethan E. Bickelhaupt

SUMMARY. This review article examines the incidence of alcoholism, and insofar as possible, other forms of drug abuse, among gays and lesbians in the United States and one European society. The consensus is that about 25% of such persons suffer from definitive drug and alcohol abuse problems, while an additional percentage experience "suggestive or problematic" abuse patterns.

INTRODUCTION

Clinicians treating gay and lesbian Americans have long suspected that the incidence of alcoholism and other forms of chemical dependency in this population is higher than for the population in general. But does the research support this suspicion, or is the suspicion based solely on impressions from clinical practice? In this article, seven research studies which seek to identify the incidence

Ethan E. Bickelhaupt, MD, FAPA, a physician who specializes in family practice, psychiatry, and addiction medicine in Perry and Topeka, Kansas, is a Diplomat of the American Board of Psychiatry and Neurology, certified by the American Society of Addiction Medicine, and a Fellow of the American Psychiatric Association.

Address correspondence to Dr. Bickelhaupt at P.O. Box 2033, Topeka, KS 66601 USA.

[Haworth co-indexing entry note]: "Alcoholism and Drug Abuse in Gay and Lesbian Persons: A Review of Incidence Studies." Bickelhaupt, Ethan E. Co-published simultaneously in *Journal of Gay & Lesbian Social Services* (The Haworth Press, Inc.) Vol. 2, No. 1, 1995, pp. 5-14: and: *Addiction and Recovery in Gay and Lesbian Persons* (ed: Robert J. Kus) The Haworth Press, Inc., 1995, pp. 5-14. Multiple copies of this article/chapter may be purchased from The Haworth Document Delivery Center [1-800-3-HAWORTH; 9:00 a.m. - 5:00 p.m. (EST)].

of chemical dependency or chemical abuse in gay and lesbian persons will be explored. Six of the studies were conducted in the United States, and one was conducted in the Czech Republic. These studies (Fifield, 1975; Kelly, 1991; Kus and Procházka, 1991; Lohrenz et al., 1978; Morales and Graves, 1983; Mosbacher, 1993; and Saghir and Robins, 1973) show that between 20-35% of gay and lesbian adults suffer from alcoholism, have a drinking problem, or use illegal, mind-altering drugs. Because this finding has many implications for clinicians, researchers, and gay and lesbian community leaders, it would be wise to explore each of these studies in terms of what each found.

FINDINGS

The Fifield Study (1975)

Fifield (1975) provided an analysis of alcohol abuse and an evaluation of alcoholism rehabilitation services for the Los Angeles gay community. This analysis included investigation and documentation of the degree and nature of alcohol abuse problems within the gay community. The study was conducted by the Gay Community Services Center with support from the Department of Health Services (Central Health Services Region) of the County of Los Angeles. Questionnaires were utilized to obtain demographic information from users of Center programs, and questionnaires were sent to bartenders, bar owners, and bar users, as well as to "alcoholism recovery programs." There were around 500 respondents in all subject categories. The average age for the gay problem drinker was 35 years, with an average annual income of under $8,000 and "some college."

Using the "bartenders' estimate," 10-16% of the total gay population in Los Angeles County were found to be "alcohol abusers" or "problem drinkers." By using the "bar users' self-report estimate," the percentage increased to 32%. A startling 48% of gay bar users exceeded a "blood alcohol content" (B.A.C.) of 0.10 on an "average evening." This estimate was based on consuming six or more alcoholic drinks for that evening.

The Kelly Study (1991)

The Kelly study (1991) looked at incidence as part of a larger study that also examined the availability of chemical dependency treatment services and the implications of incidence in relation to such services or the lack thereof. The sample included gay, lesbian, and bisexual persons in the San Francisco area and totaled 748 individuals. Of these 44% were women, 77% were white, 73% were employed, and 87% had some college education. Study methods for the incidence portion of the research involved a 209-item AOD (alcohol and other drug use) survey distributed throughout the gay, lesbian, and bisexual community in San Francisco over a two-month period. This distribution was accomplished using a gay/lesbian monthly newspaper, bookstores, businesses, organizations, service agencies, personal networks of LAGSAP (Lesbian and Gay Substance Abuse Planning Group), and field workers. In addition there were interviews with targeted populations, including people of color, youth, and homeless or low income people.

In the Kelly research nearly one-third (31%) of gay and bisexual men reported using alcohol and/or drugs at the highest risk level established for their survey, likely reflecting chemical dependency or addiction. Another 11% reported such abuse in the next highest risk category, suggesting "problematic" patterns of alcohol and drug use. Thus, up to 42% of gay and bisexual men may currently be using alcohol and other drugs at risky or problematic levels.

Other major findings of the Kelly study were that rates of alcohol and other drug use, while consistently higher than in the general population, were somewhat lower than in previous gay/lesbian studies. Alcohol was clearly the drug of choice for both men (75%) and women (66%). Forty percent of male and 30% of female alcohol users reported using at least one other drug occasionally. About one-half used alcohol several times a month or more. Men who used alcohol daily did so at a rate twice that of women (approximately 10% vs. 5.5%).

Marijuana was the second most common drug used, with 50% of the men and 38% of the women reporting use within the past year. Women used pot at a slightly higher rate than did men (13% vs. 11%). Inhalants, primarily amyl nitrate, were the next most frequently used drugs for gay and bisexual men, used by 27%, compared to 3% for women. Painkillers, including analgesics, barbiturates, opiates, and others, were the third most frequently used in women and the fourth in men. Amphetamines, tranquilizers, and cocaine were used by gay and bisexual men at a rate of 17.5%. Women use cocaine and tranquilizers at a rate of about 15%. Both groups were similar in their use of hallucinogens (10%), barbiturates (4%), and heroin and other opiates (4%). Women amphetamine users were at nine percent. Seven percent of men and three percent of women used crack cocaine. About one-third of men and one-fourth of women smoked cigarettes.

The Kus and Procházka Study (1991)

The Kus and Procházka study (1991) set out to identify the incidence of alcoholism among gay Czechoslovak men. One hundred gay men were selected through network sampling by the co-author (Procházka), who recruited men from the health services at Charles University, from members of Prague's gay group, or from friends of these men. The study was conducted in Prague, the capitol of the Czech Republic, and was part of a larger five-nation study which was also examining many other dimensions of gay men's lives, including their knowledge, beliefs, and attitudes on a variety of issues. In the Czechoslovak sample, ages ranged from under 20 to under 60; 35% were coupled, eight percent were married, and 57% were single. The majority were not particularly religious; most had gone to high school or beyond. Occupations were varied, with professionals being "over-represented" and incomes average to above.

The MAST (Michigan Alcoholism Screening Test), written in Czech, was used to identify alcoholism in the Kus and Procházka study. The MAST is a 25-item questionnaire, each item weighted from one to five points. This test was modified for the Czech society and its gay sample. If a man answered affirmative to being alcoholic prior to the screen, the MAST was omitted, and he was listed as alcoholic for research purposes.

In the Kus and Procházka study 22% were found to be "definitely alcoholic," scoring five or more on the MAST, while another six to fifteen percent (with the variance attempting to account for cultural bias) were found to be "suggestive of alcoholism," scoring four points. Sixty-three percent were noted to be non-alcoholic. The 22% figure is similar to that found in gay American men, while a 28%-37% range of "positively or likely alcoholic" finding in gay Czech men is higher than what has been typically found in their American counterparts.

The Lohrenz et al. Study (1978)

The purpose of the Lohrenz et al. study (1978) was to examine both the nature and extent of alcohol problems in four urban areas in Kansas, as well as the attitudes of homosexual alcoholics toward traditional mental health resources and Alcoholics Anonymous (A.A.). One hundred forty-five gay men were ultimately studied; 29 women were omitted due to small sample size. A 73-item questionnaire was used, including the entire Michigan Alcoholism Screening Test (MAST). It was distributed by leaders of three homosexual communities, by mailings to several regional homosexual organizations, and by distributing them at a university homosexual dance and at several homosexual bars. Most of the men were young (18-35 year age group), from medium-sized or larger cities (10,000 to 100,000 or more), and were generally well-educated.

The most striking finding was that 29% of the men surveyed were categorized as alcoholics by the MAST. The mean score of those categorized as alcoholics was 12.7, a very high mean score, while the range was five to 50. The percentage itself compares closely to the findings of the Fifield study.

The Morales and Graves Study (1983)

The Morales and Graves study (1983) had a two-fold purpose: to examine the extent of substance abuse within the gay and lesbian community in San Francisco and to assess various characteristics of the substance abuse providers within county-funded drug treatment programs. The incidence portion of the study was designed to assess the incidence of alcohol and other drug use among lesbians and gay men in San Francisco. The sample included a total of 453 persons who completed questionnaires, 266 (59%) of whom were gay males and 129 (28%) of whom were lesbians. Fifty-seven (13%) were bisexual or "gay-identified heterosexuals" in various stages of "coming out," etc. Because of the small size and mixed membership of these latter groups, they were not included in the final analysis of the results. Members of ethnic minority groups comprised about 14% of the total sample, and the mean age was about 33 years old. About 15% were unemployed, while those employed tended to be in service-oriented or business occupations. Income averages were $12,000 per year for lesbians and $18,000 for gay men and bisexuals. Educational differences were unremarkable, with the average numbers of school years completed being fifteen among all groups. Sixty percent of lesbians and 40% of gay men were coupled.

Self-administered questionnaires, including the frequency of substance use and preferred methods for administration, were distributed for a six week period to a variety of gay and lesbian community organizations, persons on the street in the Castro district, prisoners in the county jail system, and through assistance of the Department of Public Health and the Gay and Lesbian Task Force on Substance Abuse networks.

The results of the Morales and Graves study reveal that 18% of gay men and nearly 25% of lesbians presented an "at risk" substance abuse pattern, while 21% of gay and lesbian ethnic minorities seemed to have significant drug-related problems. These percentages were thought to be conservative, based on their estimates from negative drug and alcohol-related experiences and in light of the demographic variables between the gay men and lesbians. Alcohol was used by the largest number of subjects in both the lesbian and gay men groups when contrasted to other drugs. Twenty-eight percent of gay men, 27% of lesbians, and 21% of ethnic group members used alcohol one or more times daily. Eighty-three percent of gay men and 76% of lesbians reported use of alcohol in the twelve months prior to study participation. Slightly fewer subjects in these two groups indicated that they had smoked marijuana or hashish during the same period. Only the ethnic minorities reported using more marijuana or hashish (79%) than alcohol (76%), with alcohol and marijuana comprising the primary and secondary drugs of choice respectively for all groups. Over 50% of all subjects reported cocaine use during the one year prior to the study, while cocaine was the second drug of choice for all lesbians and ethnic minority participants. More gay men (57.5%) reported use of nitrites than use of cocaine (52%), while nitrite use was markedly lower in all other groups. For eight other drugs studied, gay men generally had higher proportions of substance abuse than did lesbians. Both used quaaludes and mushrooms about equally (27% and 20% respectively). The largest differences between gay men and lesbians were related to their respective use of MDA (22% vs. 8.5%), of LSD (17% vs. 14%), and of methamphetamines (21% vs. 12%).

The Saghir and Robins Study (1973)

The purpose of the Saghir and Robins study (1973) was broad in scope and attempted to describe the natural history of homosexuality, focusing primarily on a descriptive presentation of the behavioral manifestations and correlates of homosexuality. The use and abuse of alcohol and other drugs were examined in both "male and female homosexuals" as part of their look at "psychopathology."

The samples were obtained with the solicited help of homophile organizations in Chicago and San Francisco through direct appeal during their regular meetings and by "word of mouth" to other members and friends. The criteria for inclusion were self-reported homosexual orientation and continued homosexual activity beyond age 18. The criteria for exclusion were present or past psychiatric hospitalizations, history of imprisonment, and being non-white. A total of 89 homosexual men and 57 homosexual women participated. The age range of the men was 19-70 years with a mean and a median close to 34. Eighty-two percent were "single." Socioeconomic status was generally high. For the women the age range was 20-54 years with a mean of 31 years. Over 75% had never been married. Socioeconomic status again was high.

The data for the entire study, including the portion on substance abuse, were derived from structured clinical interviews lasting three to four hours and with most questions answered by "yes" or "no" or by a number, although some were open-ended. Alcoholism was diagnosed if symptoms were found in at least three of four possible groups as described by Guze et al. (1963) on "the drinking history."

Seventy percent of the men never drank alcohol or were mild drinkers. Eleven percent (11%) were diagnosed to be alcoholic, while another 19% were found to be "problem drinkers." Among women 65% were mild drinkers or teetotalers, while 25% were "problem drinkers" and 10% were alcoholics.

Thirty-nine percent of homosexual men reported using one or more illicit drugs, with the breakdown as follows: eight percent used marijuana only; 10% used amphetamines; nine percent used barbiturates, hallucinogens, opiates, or amyl nitrite. Twelve percent of the men used a combination of these drugs. Among the homosexual women, 51% reported using non-prescription drugs, mostly marijuana and amphetamines. Five women used barbiturates alone or in addition to marijuana, amphetamines, hallucinogens or amyl nitrite. The remaining 24 women who used illicit drugs experimented only, with marijuana, amphetamines, or a combination of both. As with the males, a majority (55%) of the females who were drug users drank excessively.

The Mosbacher Study (1993)

The Mosbacher study (1993) was undertaken to compare rates of substance abuse among lesbian, female heterosexual, and bisexual medical students. The bisexual group was ultimately dropped from consideration due to small sample size. About 400 questionnaires were distributed to female attendees at the 1986 American Medical Student Association (AMSA) in New Orleans, LA, and another 100 questionnaires were mailed to 100 female medical students on the Lesbian, Bisexual, and Gay People in Medicine Task Force of the American Medical Student Association. From these, 308 study participants were selected after completing a 51-item questionnaire, containing three questions about sexual orientation. The sample represented all geographic regions in the U.S., with 86% being white and 64% having a modal age less than 28 years. The modal income was between $10,000 and $19,000 annually. About 11% of the sample were lesbians and 85% female heterosexuals, with the remaining percentage being bisexual and too small to consider for study purposes. Forty percent of the respondents reported that a family member had an alcohol or drug problem.

The remaining items of the above questionnaire assessed the use and abuse of alcohol and other drugs utilizing the Short Michigan

Alcohol Screening Test (SMAST). The SMAST is an abbreviated form of the MAST, used to estimate the prevalence of alcohol abuse, and consisting of 13 "yes/no" questions, which are scored 0-1 according to the responses. A total score of two (2) points is considered suggestive of alcohol or drug dependency. A score of greater than or equal to three (3) is considered dependence. The SMAST was also adapted to assess abuse of other drugs by asking respondents to select, from a list of 11 drugs, the two with which they had the most experience.

The results of the Mosbacher study (1993) revealed that the mean SMAST scores for both groups for drugs and alcohol were less than two (2) points. However, abuse for both alcohol and drugs was much higher among lesbians, noting that nearly 40% of them scored two or higher on the Alcohol SMAST, compared to 17% of their heterosexual counterparts. In the high-risk category of abuse (3 or more), 18% of the lesbians were represented, while only four percent of heterosexuals were in this category. Although the drug SMAST scores were lower than the alcohol scores, lesbians were much more often in the high-risk category for abuse, noting six percent of lesbians compared to one percent of heterosexuals with scores of three or higher. Those who scored two or more on the SMAST included 12% of lesbians and almost six percent of heterosexuals, i.e., those at "some risk."

Five percent of the heterosexual women and six percent of the lesbians did not drink. Among those who did drink, levels of alcohol use were similar for both groups, with four to six drinks per week as the mode. The top two drugs of choice for both lesbians and heterosexuals were amphetamines and barbiturates. Lesbians were much more likely to use drugs (39%) than their heterosexual counterparts (21.5%).

DISCUSSION

While it is difficult to compare these various incidence studies directly due to varying samples and methodologies, it is clear that somewhere between one-fifth to one-third of gay men (here and abroad) and lesbians use alcohol in a problematic fashion. The actual incidence of the problematic use of other drugs is harder to ascertain, but the report from the Morales and Graves study (1983) that as many as 50% of gays and lesbians used cocaine within the past one year is striking, even if it is assumed that not all use is deemed problematic.

Further research into the problem of chemical dependency in gay and lesbian persons is essential, essential for gay and lesbian persons themselves, for those who love them, for their community leaders, and for clinicians who treat them. The days of basing treatment or policy decisions solely on anecdotal data are gone. Today we need solid scientific research. The implications of chemical dependency are too great to be left to folk theories.

REFERENCES

1. Fifield, L. (1975). *On my way to nowhere: Alienated, isolated, drunk.* Los Angeles: Gay Community Services Center and Department of Health Services, County of Los Angeles.

2. Guze, S.B., Tuason, V.B., Stewart, M.A. and Picken, B. (1963). The drinking history: A comparison of reports by subjects and their relatives. *Q. J. Stud. Alcohol, 24,* 249-260.

3. Kelly, J. (Ed.) (1991). *San Francisco lesbian, gay and bisexual alcohol and other drugs needs assessment study: Vol. 1.* Sacramento, CA: EMT Associates, Inc.

4. Kus, R.J. and Procházka, I. (1991, June). *Alcoholism in gay Czechoslovak men: An incidence study.* Paper presented at the 36th International Institute on the Prevention and Treatment of Alcoholism, Stockholm, Sweden.

5. Lohrenz, L., Connelly, J., Coyne, L., and Spare, K. (1978). Alcohol problems in several midwestern homosexual communities. *Journal of Studies on Alcohol, 39,* 1959-1963.

6. Morales, E.S. and Graves, M.A. (1983). *Substance abuse: Patterns and barriers to treatment for gay men and lesbians in San Francisco.* San Francisco: San Francisco Prevention Resources Center.

7. Mosbacher, D. (1993). Alcohol and other drug use in female medical students: A comparison of lesbians and heterosexuals. *Journal of Gay and Lesbian Psychotherapy, 2*(1) 37-48.

8. Saghir, M. and Robins, E. (1973). *Male and female homosexuality.* Baltimore: Williams and Wilkins.

Chemical Dependency and HIV Infection

Melvin I. Pohl

SUMMARY. In the United States, AIDS has affected gay men more than any social group. There are special relationships between drug dependency and HIV infection/AIDS. Any discussion of the special needs of chemically dependent gay and lesbian persons must include the special problems clinicians need to be aware of when caring for the HIV-positive patient. This article explores HIV disease including its causes, development, transmission, treatments, and effects.

INTRODUCTION

In the 1990s, no discussion of chemical dependency can omit information about HIV infection and AIDS. AIDS is the most serious epidemic facing our society today. AIDS was first recognized in a group of gay men in 1981, and since that time more than 300,000 cases have been reported nationwide with more than 150,000 deaths. Worldwide there are over 2,000,000 reported cases of AIDS with 13,000,000 people estimated to be infected. The World Health Organization projects that by the year 2000 there will be 40,000,000 to over a 100,000,000 people infected with HIV, 10,000,000 of

Melvin I. Pohl, MD, author and physician, is a family practitioner and Clinical Director of Addiction Services at Montevista Hospital in Las Vegas and Medical Director of Substance Abuse Services at Behavioral Healthcare Options in Las Vegas.

Address correspondence to Dr. Pohl at 2800 Cowan Circle, Las Vegas, NV 89107.

[Haworth co-indexing entry note]: "Chemical Dependency and HIV Infection." Pohl, Melvin I. Co-published simultaneously in *Journal of Gay & Lesbian Social Services* (The Haworth Press, Inc.) Vol. 2, No. 1, 1995, pp. 15-28: and: *Addiction and Recovery in Gay and Lesbian Persons* (ed: Robert J. Kus) The Haworth Press, Inc., 1995, pp. 15-28. Multiple copies of this article/chapter may be purchased from The Haworth Document Delivery Center [1-800-3-HAWORTH; 9:00 a.m. - 5:00 p.m. (EST)].

whom will be infants. Recently, the Center for Disease Control has expanded the case definition for AIDS, increasing the number of cases identified as AIDS in the United States (CDC, 1986; CDC, 1987; CDC, 1992).

The demographics of the epidemic have been changing over time, with increasing cases in heterosexuals and IV drug addicts. Fifty-nine percent of the cases in the United States, however, still occur in gay men with an additional 7% in gay IV drug addicts (Schoenbaum et al., 1989). Therefore, the AIDS epidemic is intimately involved in the lives of most gay men and many lesbians. AIDS may impact the process of recovery in the following ways:

1. Gay men entering chemical dependency treatment may be HIV-positive or have AIDS.
2. Gay men entering chemical dependency treatment are at risk for HIV and AIDS because of sexual behavior engaged in while intoxicated.
3. All IV drug addicts entering treatment are at risk for infection if they have been exposed to needles containing HIV.
4. Many gay men and lesbians have lost numbers of friends and lovers to AIDS.

This chapter will discuss the nature of Human Immunodeficiency Virus (HIV), transmission of this virus, testing, treatment, and psychosocial considerations as they relate to chemically dependent lesbian and gay people.

AIDS AND HIV INFECTION

AIDS is an underlying disorder of the immune system caused by Human Immunodeficiency Virus (HIV). In individuals who become infected, HIV acts as a slow, silent virus. HIV has a propensity to infect certain cells of the body whose function is to fight off infection and cancers. One of the primary targets of HIV is the T-4 lymphocyte or CD-4 cell, a type of white blood cell specifically charged with organizing the sophisticated functions of the immune system.

After penetrating the T-4 cell, the genetic material of HIV becomes incorporated into the genetic material of the human cell and may lay dormant for many years. Eventually, many people go from an asymptomatic condition into one characterized by progressive loss of T-4 cells, resulting in decreased efficiency of the immune system's ability to fight off infections and cancers.

To actually be diagnosed with AIDS, a patient, in addition to having evidence of HIV infection, must have one of the following:

1. Presumptive or proven opportunistic infection including those caused by protozoa, virus, fungus, and certain bacteria;
2. One of several forms of cancer, specifically lymphoma, cancer of the cervix, or Kaposi's sarcoma;
3. HIV encephalopathy (problems with thinking, judgement, memory, mood, and other brain functions) with resulting cognitive dysfunction, caused by HIV infection of the brain;
4. Wasting syndrome with weight loss, fever, diarrhea; or
5. Less than 200 T-4 cells. (CDC, 1992)

The clinical course of HIV infection varies over time in different people. Initially infection appears as a viral illness with fever, swollen glands, body aches and a rash. Many people infected with HIV remain asymptomatic for many years. Subsequently, approximately 50% of people over ten years, according to one study (Moss et al., 1988), go on and develop more serious signs and symptoms of infection, including fevers, night sweats, diarrhea, mild infections such as thrush, weight loss, swollen glands, fatigue, and eventually progressive serious and debilitating illness, as described above. The worst cases of AIDS eventually cause disability and death; many people live fairly healthy lives for many years.

Transmission

HIV is spread between humans through intimate sexual contact (by entry of semen or vaginal fluid into the blood stream) or by the exchange of blood (entry of blood into the blood stream). There is not enough virus present in tears, saliva or sweat to permit transmission of this virus between people. Even if enough virus were present in these fluids, direct access to the blood stream is required before infection with HIV can occur. To date, no cases have been reported of infection with HIV through casual contact, even in studies of family members who have shared eating utilities, bathrooms and common household areas (Friedland & Klein, 1987).

Because HIV is found in blood, sharing an intravenous drug injecting apparatus is a very efficient way of transmitting the virus. Injecting drugs, particularly intravenous cocaine, puts the drug addict in great danger of becoming infected with HIV, especially if he/she is in an environment with other addicts injecting (Chaisson et al., 1989). Transmission reduction techniques, including the "harm reduction model" practiced in many cities in Europe, involve a hierarchical approach to risk reduction and may be applicable to lesbian and gay chemically dependent clients (Cates, 1992):

1. Abstinence from all mood altering drugs through treatment is optimal.
2. If a person is unwilling or unable to become abstinent, eliminating needles would be a reasonable goal. In methadone maintenance programs, there is a lower rate of HIV infection associated with being in treatment (Cooper, 1989). Unfortunately, amphetamine and cocaine addicts do not benefit from maintenance drugs at this time.
3. Injecting, but not sharing needles, is the next level in the model. Making needles available more readily, as with needle exchange programs, may result in decreased transmission of HIV. Preliminary studies have provided evidence that HIV in needles being returned went down over time (Stimson, 1989; O'Keefe et al., 1991).
4. If sharing a needle, sterilizing the needle with 10% bleach may be effective in killing the virus. However, the efficiency of viral eradication is not 100% with this method (Vlahov et al., 1991).

It is felt that through such an approach, eventually in an appropriate system, intravenous drug users may progress through the hierarchy and eventually stop using drugs altogether. In the interim, the incidence of HIV will be substantially decreased by these measures.

The second way HIV is transmitted in the gay community is through sexual contact. It appears that passive rectal sex (penis inserted into the rectum) is an efficient way of transmitting HIV.

Semen containing HIV comes in contact with an abraded rectal mucosa. There are safer sex techniques available which are relatively efficient at decreasing HIV transmission. Studies have demonstrated that despite knowledge and prior safer sex practices, people who used drugs (drank two alcoholic beverages or smoked one marijuana cigarette) didn't practice safer sex techniques which they were taught previously (Coates & Stall, 1988). Crack cocaine also places people at an increased risk of practicing unsafe sex due to increased libido and disinhibition secondary to dopamine stimulation (Chaisson et al., 1991; Fullilove et al., 1990).

Finally, there is evidence that T-cells of people who drank alcohol the previous night were more readily infected by HIV (Bagasra, 1989); HIV replication in T-4 cells was 1,000 times greater in cells after exposure to cocaine in the test tube than in nonexposed cells (Bagasra et al., 1989). This phenomenon indicates that anyone who uses alcohol and other drugs may be at increased risk for infection with HIV when exposed, and is at increased risk of HIV replication after ingesting cocaine. Alcohol and cocaine, as well as perhaps marijuana, opiates and PCP, may either damage the body's immune system or stimulate HIV in such a way as to make HIV's effect on the body more damaging (Macdonald, 1987). Alcohol and other drugs then become "co-factors" that combine with HIV to cause damage to the immune system. To date, however, studies have failed to prove that HIV disease progresses faster in intravenous drug users (IVDUs) (Margolic et al., 1992).

In the gay culture, some studies indicate a high incidence of alcohol and drug problems (Kus & Procházka, 1991; Lohrenz et al., 1978; McKirnan & Peterson, 1989; Morales & Graves, 1983; Saghir & Robins, 1973). There is clearly a connection between drug problems and HIV infection, especially in gay men who do not practice safer sex.

Testing

Currently, technology is available to assess HIV antibody levels to detect the presence of viral particles (antigens) in the human blood stream. The primary method for testing for antibodies is the Elisa test. Samples that react to the Elisa test are then tested with a more sophisticated blood test called the Western Blot, which confirms the presence of antibodies to HIV. Because there is a substantial incidence of false positive Elisa tests, it is essential to confirm any positive Elisa with a Western Blot test. HIV antibodies usually appear within six (6) weeks of infection and are most always present by 6 months post-infection (Lazzarin et al., 1991).

Antigen usually appears within a few weeks of infection and disappears within a few months. Later, if the virus is activated, the dormancy ends and the antigen level rises. A rising antigen level is typically associated with deterioration of a person's physical condition and may herald the development of AIDS in a person who had been previously asymptomatic (Allain et al., 1987). Antigen testing is not yet routinely available and is still being standardized for interpretation.

Since most sexually active gay men are potentially at risk for HIV infection, it would be best for them to know their HIV status. The main reasons for knowing one's HIV status are to facilitate treatment and to prevent transmission. Many clinicians, expert in treating this special population, suggest that all men who have had sex with men consider themselves already infected by the virus. Since they are assumed to have been infected, it is recommended that gay and bi-sexual men refrain from donating blood, sperm, and organs, always practice safer sex, and boost their health and nutritional status through proper exercise and diet (a form of "universal precaution").

It is important to confirm the presence of HIV antibodies and presumed HIV infection by taking an antibody test as soon as it is safe and feasible. The decision point to do HIV testing is still a difficult one and should be individualized. In the drug and alcohol treatment setting, the rationale for deferral of testing coincides with a system's inability to respond effectively to patients' needs if they are tested. Programs need to find their own balance between the positives and negatives of early voluntary testing of individuals within their patient population.

Since there are early treatment interventions possible, there has been a shift towards earlier detection of HIV infection. However, there are risks to HIV testing, especially with inadequate preparation for such testing. Assessments should focus special attention on clients who are not stable in treatment, many of whom are at risk for relapsing to drug use or becoming suicidal after being diagnosed as HIV positive (Marzuk et al., 1988).

Optimal treatment for any person with any illness would dictate thorough assessment, diagnosis and compilation of a medical record that included the assessment and diagnostic workup. When it comes to considering assessment, diagnostic testing and documentation of information regarding HIV illness, certain other considerations must be made. People who are HIV-positive are subject to many forms of discrimination with respect to housing, job, child custody, and insurance benefits. Therefore, the assessment, diagnosis and documentation process for information about HIV positivity ought to be carefully considered and formalized in hospital and office policies and procedures. If confidentiality can be ensured, then it would be appropriate to order and document proper diagnostic procedures, specifically HIV antibody testing and results. If there is a question about the ability to ensure the confidentiality of this information, consideration ought to be given for alternatives including off-site testing with no information in the chart, on-site testing with no information in the chart (information provided in a separate unnamed and confidential chart) or testing without entering obvious information into the medical record about HIV infection (e.g., "test results positive" rather than "HIV antibody results positive"). Each of the latter two procedures would require specific mechanisms to institute and ensure compliance (Gayle & Ostrow, 1986).

If a facility enters information routinely in the chart, it might be appropriate and beneficial to meet with the patient, explain the possible implications of charting such information, and have the patient sign a consent form. Obviously, all of these activities ought to be done when the patient is cognitively intact and able to understand the significance of such decisions rather than during the detox period when under the influence of or withdrawing from mood-altering drugs.

Handling this information in the patient community presents similar complex questions. Though secrets are unhealthy for CD patients in general, disclosure of HIV status may not be met with support. Individualized decisions must be facilitated by knowledgeable staff in the treatment setting.

TREATMENT

Goals of treatment for all people who are HIV-positive are to:

a. prevent disease transmission,
b. decrease viral replication,
c. boost the immune system,
d. enhance quality of life.

Treatment of HIV infection and AIDS is becoming progressively more sophisticated resulting in:

a. longer life for people with AIDS;
b. slowed progression of HIV infection into AIDS;
c. prolonged and improved quality of life as a result of better treatments for opportunistic infections and cancers.

In 1985, the average life span for somebody diagnosed with AIDS was 9 months. By 1989, 61% of people with AIDS were alive 18 months after diagnosis, signifying increased efficacy of intervention strategies for AIDS and opportunistic infections associated with AIDS. There is much encouraging and promising research being undertaken on all fronts of AIDS treatment.

We can break treatment methodology into four categories:

1. antiviral;
2. immunomodulators and/or stimulators;
3. treatments for opportunistic infection;
4. prophylaxis against opportunistic infection.

The prototype *antiviral* is zidovudine (formally known as AZT). Zidovudine (or Retrovir) and other antiretrovirals attack the virus by halting its ability to reproduce or transcribe itself (by inhibiting reverse transcriptase). The other RT inhibitors include DDI (Didanosine), DDC (Dideoxycytidine) and D4T (Stavudine). Zidovudine has been approved as first line treatment of AIDS and has been shown to prolong life in people with AIDS (Graham et al., 1992). DDI is approved for use if AZT is not working or is toxic. DDC is approved for use in combination with AZT for more efficacious antiviral effect.

D4T is available under an experimental "expanded access program" at the time of this writing for people who are unable to tolerate AZT.

Immunomodulators stimulate T-cells and other immune system components to enable the system to more effectively fight off infection. These include interferon and other experimental substances. The status of vaccinations as part of treatment is also being studied. Some vaccines seem to be effective in boosting immune function in people who are already infected. Ultimately, scientists are hopeful about creating a vaccine that will prevent infection.

Opportunistic Infections. There are many excellent drugs available to treat the variety of infections that take the opportunity to attack the patient with an impaired system. In the last three (3) years at least ten (10) drugs have been introduced for this purpose. There are many others in the process of being investigated which will probably be released over the next several years. Pneumocystis pneumonia is still the most common infection and can be treated with any of three (3) drugs (sulfa, pentamidine, or atovquone) (Kovacs & Masur, 1988). A new infection causing great concern is a form of tuberculosis that resists treatment with standard anti-tuberculous medications (Monno et al., 1991). There are also excellent treatments for fungal, bacterial, protozoal, and viral infections such as herpes and cytomegalovirus as well as for various cancers (radiation and chemotherapy).

Prophylaxis. Current standard of care includes preventive treatment for anyone with a T-4 count under 2-300 with sulfa drugs or, as an alternative, pentamidine (CDC, 1989). There are also prophylactic protocols against certain fungal, viral, and protozoal infections which are being studied.

Psychosocial Issues

Solomon and Temoshok (Temoshok et al., 1990; Pivar et al., 1990) studied long-term survivors with AIDS. They identified certain characteristics correlated with survival including assertiveness, accepting the diagnosis and reality, having a positive attitude, taking personal responsibility for life, having a sense of purpose with commitment to life, collaborating with the treatment team, being able to nurture self, working with others who are infected, and being emotionally connected with others (Callen, 1990). Therefore, enhancing immune function and quality of life correlates with strategies that will reinforce the behaviors listed above.

It is probably no coincidence that these behaviors and characteristics correlate almost exactly with characteristics of recovery from chemical dependency. 12-step programs are excellent vehicles to enhance life and the chance of survival after persons are diagnosed with HIV infection and AIDS.

Treatment of patients with the dual diagnosis of HIV/AIDS and chemical dependency is much more complex than treatment of patients who are uninfected with HIV. Issues that come up for treatment professionals include fear from the patient, society, other treatment professionals and communities of patients. Fear about AIDS is at times irrational, but it is necessary to deal with and attempt to work through this fear. There is a deep-seated prejudice against people with HIV infection as well as against gay men and lesbians. Therefore, issues of stigma, blame and guilt will dominate the recovery from both illnesses. Lastly, grief and fatalism about an HIV diagnosis often will interfere with the treatment process. The patient's ability to work on recovery in the face of a potentially terminal illness often is impaired.

It is common for lesbian or gay HIV-positive chemically dependent people to feel unique in a community of people who are neither HIV positive nor lesbian or gay. This uniqueness must be overcome in order for the gay or lesbian HIV patient to recover. There are symptoms that some HIV-positive people may have including pain, depression, numbness, fatigue, nausea, and fever. Many HIV-positive people will be anxious and fearful of their illness and its possible progression. It will be important to individualize treatment planning and medication usage in order to balance sobriety with comfort. Because of the complications dually diagnosed patients face, there may be an increased tendency to relapse in the face of increased life stressors. Relapse prevention is an integral part of treatment of gay chemically dependent HIV-positive patients.

Families of gay and lesbian patients with HIV infection who are chemically dependent need specialized attention as well. The issues of fear, guilt and shame, grief and loss, and sex come up for gay couples with this infection. Furthermore, families have their own needs for treatment of codependent behaviors that may exceed the codependency observed with the families of most chemically dependent people (Pohl, Kay & Toft, 1990).

Clearly, treatment of gay men and lesbians who are chemically dependent is a challenge to the chemical dependency practitioner. When those patients are infected by HIV, the treatment process becomes more complicated and often more difficult. There are many accepted treatment techniques to deal with these patients, many of which have been described in this article. CD professionals working with these populations must individualize their care, be flexible, be knowledgeable about HIV infection and AIDS, and provide heartfelt caring and support. Patients with these diagnoses are taxing, and clinicians may need to call upon other professionals to monitor their own needs to guard against the possibility of burnout.

CONCLUSIONS

Treating gay and lesbian people who are chemically dependent is a much more complex process than treating non-gay and lesbian people. Issues of shame, stigma, uniqueness, and disclosure all complicate the process of recovery for gay men and lesbians. When dealing with HIV-infected gay or lesbian chemically dependent patients, the process becomes even more complicated. HIV exacerbates the guilt and shame, fear and sense of uniqueness that all gay and lesbian chemically dependent people feel. This article has discussed special issues that come up for gay men and lesbians who are HIV positive. Programs and therapists need to be flexible in order to individualize care for people with these different issues. Often it is a struggle for patients to focus on their chemical dependency when HIV issues come up (problems with health, relationships, fear of dying). The job of the chemical dependency professional is to balance the patient's need to process their HIV status with the clear-cut importance of developing a foundation of recovery.

The following guidelines (see Figure 1) reflect our current knowledge as to which sexual behaviors may be safer than others. The correct term for these practices is *safer* rather than *safe*, since one can never be certain of the long-term effects of any behavior, nor of other factors which affect transmission such as frequency of contact, dose of the virus, other infections, and susceptibility of the individual.

FIGURE 1. (adapted from Bay Area Physicians for Human Rights).

SAFER SEX

mutual masturbation, abstinence
dry kissing, body massage, hugging, using one's own sex toys

POSSIBLY SAFER SEX

insertive anal intercourse with a latex condom and nonoxynol 9
receptive anal intercourse with a latex condom and nonoxynol 9
fellatio (sucking) before climax–oral-penile or oral-vaginal
    (safer with a condom, or dental dam)
wet kissing
vaginal intercourse with a latex condom and nonoxynol 9
body contact with urine or feces

PROBABLY UNSAFE

receptive or insertive anal or vaginal intercourse without a condom
fellatio without a condom, especially with climax
oral-anal contact (rimming)
swallowing urine or feces

REFERENCES

Allain, J.P., Laurian, Y., Paul, A., Verroust, F., Lenther, M., Gazengel, C., Senn, D., Larrieu, M.-J., & Bosser, C. (1987). Long-term evaluation of HIV antigen and antibodies to p24 and gp41 in patients with hemophilia. *New England Journal of Medicine,* 317, 1114-1121.

Bagasra, O., & Formon, L. (1989). Functional analysis of lymphocyte subpopulations in experimental cocaine abuse: 1. dose-dependent activation of lymphocyte subsets. *Clinical and Experimental Immunology,* 77, 289-293.

Bagasra, O. et al. (1989). Effects of acute alcohol ingestion on in vitro susceptibility of peripheral blood mononuclear cells to infection with HIV and of selected T-cell functions. *Alcoholism: Clinical and Experimental Research,* 13, 536.

Callen, M. (1990). *Surviving AIDS.* New York: Harper Perennial.

Cates, W., & Hinmann, A. (1992). AIDS and absolutism–The demand for perfection in prevention. *New England Journal of Medicine,* 327, (7) 492-494.

Centers for Disease Control. (1986). Classification system for human T-lymphotropic virus type III/lymphadenopathy-associated virus infections. *Morbidity and Mortality Weekly Report*, 35, 334-9.

Centers for Disease Control. (1987). Council of State and Territorial Epidemiologists; AIDS Program, Centers for Infectious Diseases. Revision of the CDC surveillance case definition for acquired immunodeficiency syndrome. *Morbidity and Mortality Weekly Report*, 36 (Suppl 1), S-15S.

Centers for Disease Control. (1989). Guidelines for prophylaxis against *Pneumocystis carinii* pneumonia for persons infected with human immunodeficiency virus. *Morbidity and Mortality Weekly Report*, 38 (Suppl S-5), 1-9.

Centers for Disease Control. (1992). Revised classifications systems for HIV infection and expanded surveillance case definition for AIDS among adolescents and adults. *Morbidity and Mortality Weekly Report*, 41 (RR-17), 1-19.

Chaisson M.A., Stoneburner R.L., Hildebrandt D.S., Ewing W.E., Telzak E.E., & Jaffe H.W. (1991). Heterosexual transmission of HIV-1 associated with the use of smokable freebase cocaine (crack). *AIDS*, 5, 1121-6.

Chaisson R.E., Bachetti P., Osmond D., Brodie B., Sande M.A., & Moss A.R. (1989). Cocaine use and HIV infection in intravenous drug users in San Francisco. *Journal of the American Medical Association*, 261, 561-5.

Coates, T., Stall, R. et al. (1988). *AIDS 1988*, 2 (Suppl 1), 5239-5246.

Cooper, J.R. (1989). Methadone treatment and acquired immunodeficiency syndrome. *Journal of the American Medical Association*, 262, 1664-8.

Friedland, G.H., & Klein, R.S. (1987). Transmission of the human immunodeficiency virus. *New England Journal of Medicine*, 317, 1125-1135.

Fullilove R.E., Fullilove M.T., Bowser B.P., & Gross S.A. (1990). Risk of sexually transmitted disease among black adolescent crack users in Oakland and San Francisco, Calif. *Journal of the American Medical Association*, 263, 851-5.

Gayle, T.C., & Ostrow, D.G. (1986). Confidentiality of a patient's HIV antibody test in a psychiatric treatment unit. *QRB*, 256, 1768-1174.

Graham, M.B., & Zeger, Scott et al. (1992). The effects on survival of early treatment of Human Immunodeficiency Virus infection. *New England Journal of Medicine*, 326(16), 1037-1043.

Kovacs J.A., & Masur H. (1988). Pneumocystis carinii pneumonia: Therapy and prophylaxis. *J Infect Dis.*, 158, 254-259.

Kus, R.J. & Procházka, I. (1991, June). *Alcoholism in gay Czechoslovak men: An incidence study*. Paper presented at the 36th International Institute on the Prevention and Treatment of Alcoholism, Stockholm, Sweden.

Lazzarin A., Saracco A., Musicco M., & Nicolosi A. (1991). Man-to-woman sexual transmission of the human immunodeficiency virus: Risk factors related to sexual behavior, man's infectiousness, and woman's susceptibility. *Arch Intern Med*, 151, 2411-6.

Lohrenz, L., Connelly, J., Coyne, L., & Spare, K. (1978). Alcohol problems in several midwestern homosexual communities. *Journal of Studies on Alcoholism*, 39(11), 1959-1963.

Macdonald, D.I. (1987). IV drugs and AIDS–San Francisco, *Journal of the American Medical Association*, 258, 2642.

Margolic, J. et al. (1992). Changes in T-lymphocyte subsets in IVDUs with HIV-1 infection. *Journal of the American Medical Association*, 267(12), 1631-1636.

Marzuk, P.M., Tierney et al. (1988). Increased risk of suicide in persons with AIDS. *Journal of the American Medical Association*, 259, 1333-1337.

McKirnan, D.J. & Peterson, P.L. (1989). Alcohol and drug use among homosexual men and women: Epidemiology and population characteristics. *Addictive Behaviors*, 14, 545-553.

Monno L., Angarano G., Carbonara S. et al. (1991). Emergence of drug-resistant *Mycobacterium tuberculosis* in HIV-infected patients. *Lancet*, 337:852.

Morales, E.S. & Graves, M.A. (1983). *Substance abuse: Patterns and barriers to treatment for gay men and lesbians in San Francisco.* San Francisco: San Francisco Prevention Resources Center.

Moss, A.R. et al. (1988). Seropositivity for HIV and the development of AIDS or AIDS-related conditions: Three-year follow-up of the San Francisco general hospital cohort. *British Medical Journal*, 296, 745-750.

O'Keefe E., Kaplan E., & Khoshnood K. (1991). City of New Haven needle exchange program preliminary report. New Haven, Conn.: City of New Haven, July 1991, 18-28.

Pivar, I., & Temoshok, L. (1990). Coping strategies and response styles in homosexual symptomatic seropositive men. VIth International Conference on AIDS, San Francisco, CA.

Pohl, M., Kay, D., & Toft, D. (1990). *The caregivers' journey: When you love someone with AIDS.* Hazelden, Center City, MN.

Saghir, M.T. & Robins, E. (1973). *Male and female homosexuality: A comprehensive investigation.* Baltimore, MD: Williams & Wilkins.

Schoenbaum E.E., Hartel D., Selwyn P.A. et al. (1989). Factors for human immunodeficiency virus infection in intravenous drug users. *N. Eng J. Med.*, 321, 874-9.

Stimson G.V. (1989). Syringe-exchange programmes for injecting drug users. *AIDS*, 3, 253-60.

Temoshok, L., O'Leary, A. et al. (1990). Survival time in men with AIDS: Relationships with psychological coping and autonomic arousal. VIth International Conference on AIDS. San Francisco, CA.

Vlahov D., Munoz A., Celentano D.D. et al. (1991). HIV seroconversion and disinfection of injection equipment among intravenous drug users. Baltimore, Maryland. *Epidemiology*, 2, 444-6.

Homophobia:
The Heart of the Darkness

Sheppard B. Kominars

SUMMARY. For gay men and lesbians, one of the greatest obstacles to long-term sobriety is internalized homophobia–the hatred of one's homosexuality. Unless the crucial stage of self-acceptance is reached in the coming-out process, the effect of internalized homophobia is to put the recovery process in jeopardy and leave the gay, lesbian, bi-sexual addict/alcoholic at constant risk. Internalized homophobia can be successfully treated, but a more fundamental approach needs to be implemented in order to eliminate societal homophobia that is at the heart of the issue. To begin to do this, we need to understand the underlying nature of homophobia and how it manifests itself in everyday life. This article explores homophobia in America, how it impacts on the lives of everyone–gay, lesbian and straight–and how we can take action to eliminate it.

BACKGROUND

One of the greatest obstacles to long-term sobriety for gay men and lesbians is internalized homophobia. The fear of, and hatred of,

---

Sheppard B. Kominars, PhD, is a prolific author, playwright, and lecturer. He has specialized in gay and lesbian recovery issues for the past dozen years, and his latest book is *Accepting ourselves: The Twelve-Step journey of recovery from addiction for gay men and lesbians.*

Address correspondence to Dr. Kominars at 110 Lander Street, #2, San Francisco, CA 94114 USA.

[Haworth co-indexing entry note]: "Homophobia: The Heart of the Darkness." Kominars, Sheppard B. Co-published simultaneously in *Journal of Gay & Lesbian Social Services* (The Haworth Press, Inc.) Vol. 2, No. 1, 1995, pp. 29-39: and: *Addiction and Recovery in Gay and Lesbian Persons* (ed: Robert J. Kus) The Haworth Press, Inc., 1995, pp. 29-39. Multiple copies of this article/chapter may be purchased from The Haworth Document Delivery Center [1-800-3-HAWORTH; 9:00 a.m. - 5:00 p.m. (EST)].

one's homosexuality is a major cause of relapse in the recovery process of the chemically dependent gay man, lesbian and bisexual. This is well-documented in articles on the subject (Finnegan & McNally, 1987), as well as in the experience of many professionals working at recovery centers around the United States. Fortunately, in the stories of gay men and lesbians in recovery, there has been a marked decrease in internalized homophobia in recent years (Gay Council on Drinking Behavior, 1982; Kus, 1990).

While it is good news to learn that internalized homophobia can be successfully treated, it is important to face the even larger issue as to what can be done to *prevent* this condition from arising. Only by exploring the darkness in which society is presently groping will it be possible to overcome the devastation that homophobia causes in the lives of individuals everywhere.

THE WAY IT IS

During the first week after President Clinton announced his intention to issue an executive order allowing gays and lesbians to serve openly in the military, I telephoned my friend, Martha, in Ohio. Her immediate response to my offer to do a workshop on homophobia for heterosexuals was, "Remember, this is Middle America!" After hanging up the telephone, I thought about what this meant at this particular stage in the evolution of consciousness about the need for gay men and lesbians to enjoy the same rights as heterosexuals.

Like me, Martha is in recovery. She owns a bookstore and I know how sensitive she is to gay and lesbian issues in the recovering community. Two years ago, she hosted a book-signing for my book, *Accepting Ourselves: The Twelve-Step Journey of Recovery from Addiction for Gay Men and Lesbians* (Kominars, 1989). Through personal experience, Martha has become keenly aware of the obstacles standing in the path of men and women who have made the decision to recover from the dis-ease of compulsive behavior and the use of mood-altering substances.

Anger, fear, guilt, and isolation are four of the biggest obstacles blocking the way to recovery for men and women whether they are straight or gay. Working through these obstacles is central to the 12

Steps of *all* the Anonymous Programs. Homophobia activates within the individual each or all of these four basic obstacles to recovery. That is why dialogue and workshops on the subject are essential to health and well-being.

Workshop programs which will implement this dialogue are rare, and they are badly needed in this country. I say this because I have made efforts to change this situation with addiction counselors, and they have all confirmed this need.

"Silence = Death" is the message of recovery that society has learned painfully through the experience of the devastation of the Holocaust, and more recently in the tragedies in Somalia and Bosnia. People die if we take no action against oppression. Maintaining the silence about homophobia is destructive of the individual as well as of the society of which we are all members. The problem now facing us is: how to address the conscious and unconscious homophobia eating away at Americans today! Unless we confront this phobia directly, both the individual and the society will continue to endure the ravaging effects of hate, anger, guilt, fear, and isolation.

WHERE DO WE BEGIN?

"Be reasonable," I've been advised. "Don't make waves," I am counseled. "You're pushing the river!," say the wise. Resistance to dealing with the problem merely maintains the status quo everywhere. It is of grave concern to me that there has been little or no planning to develop strategies to change the way many men and women in the United States feel, think, and act about gays and lesbians. This neither makes good sense nor does it reveal leadership on the part of the churches, the schools, the "helping professions," or the government. What is at stake? Who is willing to lead the way? What will it take?

Every "phobia" is a deep-seated fear that compels the avoidance of the object that is feared. "Homophobia" is the irrational response to gay men or lesbians, or the idea of homosexuality. It is an *irrational* response, not a rational one.

Attacking the problem of homophobia irrationally results in the impasse many feel we have reached today: people shouting at each other, legislators bent on passing more laws to criminalize gay lifestyles, extremists attempting to polarize society even further with hate and violence. We are stuck with behavior that makes the disease only more virulent. A common-sense approach to exploring what it would take to change may yield some helpful insights.

When individuals behave irrationally, it is natural for others to respond in kind. This usually escalates any problem. The dynamics of the situation change, however, when we respond with acknowledgement, and without blame or attack. By putting behavior in a larger and more inclusive framework, we change the perspective by introducing options and alternatives which had not been present previously. Either/or attitudes fade and disappear in the light of this expanded, more inclusive context. The basic tool of recovery itself, honesty, is implemented with this process. The effect is, in most cases, the same as opening a door that had not been there. Once this has happened, it is possible to consider action that will make a major difference to the health and well-being of the individual as well as society.

Crucial to the undertaking is the respect for every individual's freedom to use and enjoy his and her talents and potential. Consistent with this respect is the acceptance—even the *celebration*—of whatever sexual orientation the individual has been blessed with. We will fail if we begin from guilt, or shame, or the inclination to apologize for individual differences, or the intention of sparing someone else's feelings. Acknowledging ourselves *as we are*, and allowing others the same freedom provides the baseline for change.

ENDING THE SILENCE

Efforts to end the silence which surrounds homosexuality have resulted in a direct assault on the massive denial that society has always hidden behind in order to avoid the issue. Talking openly about what has been true from the beginning of time—that gays and lesbians have always been an integral component of the world in which all men and women live and work—has put an end to the lie that everyone is heterosexual.

We have seen, in the last years, respectable, responsible individuals courageously revealing to the world that it is not the dregs, but an entire cross-section of society, that is homosexual. Along with these disclosures, activist groups have entered the political arena to demand protection and rights which would have been unthinkable a generation ago.

This may be the reason why men and women who have always depended upon silence for their comfort and self-righteous attitudes now feel threatened by the voices calling for even MORE acknowledgement and freedom for gays and lesbians. These same men and women are angry, and they are ashamed at the prospect. Exploring this anger and shame helps us to look at homophobia today without the filter of centuries of deception.

SOME MALE REALITIES

Two personal experiences will help illustrate the issue that needs to be considered. The first occurred during the summer when I was twelve years old. I went on a two-week holiday to Treasure Island, a Boy Scout camp on the Delaware River. One of the patrol leaders, a sixteen-year-old, was having problems with a 15-year-old who was always a discipline problem—even back home. The Patrol Leader threatened the scout with sexual violence if he did not behave. Both boys were heterosexual. Violence of a distinct sexual nature was the tool to force obedience. I remember being frightened; and in some part of me, I was angry.

I remember another experience when I was eight or nine years old. I used to have my hair cut at a barber shop a block away from my home. The barber lived with his wife and children above the store. Each time I went for a haircut, the barber would make me wait until last before cutting my hair. Afterwards, he insisted on taking me into a room behind his shop where he would rub his body against my back. At the time, I didn't understand what he was doing and I resisted. This did not stop him, and even though I don't remember being frightened, it certainly made me angry. I do remember being even angrier when I told my mother and father about it and they said nothing to him. To this day, I find myself very reluctant at the prospect of having my hair cut. Perhaps, as a child, I *was* more frightened than I realized.

Both cases involved heterosexuals using force–sexual violence–to control another or to gratify themselves. These incidents are not unique. I believe that few boys have been spared an experience, during the period of growing up, of being threatened, implied or real, with harm or punishment, or vanquishment by a rival, in a way that involves some kind of sexual assault. Forceful affronts to one's maleness are daily school-yard events–"pantsing" is a threat I have seen used with great humiliation for the victim. In these encounters, heterosexuals, not gay men, are the perpetrators, and the lesson is clear: sexual violence is one of the tools of coercion some men use to control or humiliate others and/or gratify themselves.

Two vivid scenes come to mind from the films *Deliverance* and *Lawrence of Arabia*; each film had pivotal incidents which brutally illustrate my point. The sexual violence of heterosexual males which is depicted in these stories is far more common than most men choose to acknowledge in their lives. Nevertheless, it is a very real part of the world in which the threat of assault by other men is much a part of the psyche of all males. There is a basis, in fact, for the fear of being treated "like a woman"–being sodomized–of being sexually invaded. This has many variations, from being degraded, subjected, humiliated and dominated, all the way to being taken hostage and raped!

Many boys engage in sex play. It may have happened that one of the other males was gay; perhaps he wasn't. There may even be a strong possibility of actual molestation by a man–usually a parent or other family member who is either straight or bi-sexual. This same boy grows up and passes beyond this play period; the experience from the past may become the source of fear about sexual orientation. Dark secrets are often created when previous traumatic experiences are not talked about. It is reasonable to suggest that the anger arising from such secrets or experiences is displaced on gay men in general (V. B. Larsen, personal communication, April, 1993; T. Moon, personal communication, April, 1993).

Mislabeling also accounts for an enormous amount of confusion in the straight world. Any boy may be called "gay" who is not being "manly" enough, not assertive or aggressive enough. The fact is that any male who seems unable to make it as a "real" man may be called "gay" without regard for his sexual orientation.

Stereotyping gestures, or speaking patterns, or voice pitch is another cause for being considered "different," "sissy."

HETEROSEXUAL WOMEN AND GAY MEN

It has been suggested that one possible reason why some heterosexual women avoid gay men is a concern that they might, if they encourage too many of these friendships, turn into a "fag-hag"–a derogatory term for a woman who panders to a gay man's need for a mother-figure. Another common attitude on the part of many heterosexual women is that gays do not like women. (When faced with this misconception, some gay men respond with the simple explanation, "I *do* like women! I just don't like going to bed with them!")

Over the past few years, several articles have been written about the growing phenomenon of straight women setting up housekeeping with gay men. Comfort, companionability and the absence of fear from sexual violence have been mentioned among the reasons for these arrangements.

Heterosexual women often have gay and lesbian friends. I have observed, however, that heterosexual men rarely have lesbian friends. It is possible that competition from them with other women may be the reason for this. Considering it from the perspective of human dynamics, when the heterosexual male is no longer the focus of female attention, the male finds himself in an unfamiliar and perhaps vulnerable role with a woman. Any discounting of masculinity–as if maleness were of no significance–often impacts directly upon a heterosexual male's self-esteem. Admittedly, there are "male-bashers" among lesbians, and "female-bashers" among gays, but this often has nothing to do with their orientation, but with their family history: reject others before you are rejected.

MALES AND VIOLENCE

Women have always been the victims of the sexual violence that has gone on for centuries. Accounts of battered wives are beginning to fill the dockets of the courts as never before because of the growing consciousness about the rights of women—even in the marriage which previously was sacrosanct as far as the husband's prerogatives!

What has not been openly admitted is that males, heterosexual and homosexual, have also been the victims of sexual violence for as long as women. We need to acknowledge this as the first step in dealing with homophobia.

Earlier, I referred to a specific circumstance on the national scene that, in itself, illustrates why it is necessary to consider homophobia from this perspective. The debate caused by President Clinton's decision to issue an executive order regarding gays in the military has been intense. "Although no one can doubt that many thousands of gay men and women have served, and continue to serve honorably and well, homophobic prejudice runs deep and wide through all four branches of the uniformed services" (Morganthau et al., Feb. 1, 1993, p. 54).

Addressing this issue, David Tuller wrote, "The ferocious debate about gays in the military can be summed up in a word: showers" (Tuller, Feb. 18, 1993, p. 1 & ff.). Straight men's fear of harassment by gays is rooted, according to Tuller, in the image of the homosexual as a predator. He goes on to say that the image of predatory gay men stems from the popularity of gay bathhouses and sex clubs in the '70s to the present—"in spite of AIDS."

This may, in part, be the case, but I do not agree that this is the *basis* for the image. Even more fundamental, it seems, is the potential for men, as a manifestation of their maleness, to use force in achieving any objective. "Many boys are never taught to say 'no,' " is the way one heterosexual put it. "Because they don't know how to say 'no,' they confront others with force if they cannot get their way." Sexual violence is one of the most powerful weapons in the entire arsenal of alternatives.

VICTIMS AND PREDATORS

Gay men and lesbians are keenly aware of what it is to be the victims of physical and emotional violence. It seems ironic, paradoxical even, that gay men and lesbians in the military or anywhere are considered to be the threat—the predators—to heterosexuals. Publicizing the statistics that most of the child-molestation in this country is done by *heterosexuals* (Berger & Kelly, 1994) addresses and corrects one of the basic criticisms used against gays and lesbians. I believe that any strategy for change starts with this acknowledgement. Starting there, we can begin to work on basic re-education about what is acceptable behavior and what is not so that it fits into a context of honesty about sex and crime which presently does not exist.

Fear and anger imprison every individual for as long as he or she chooses to endure living under their sway. At the heart of recovery is the willingness to deal with any and all obstacles. As long as violence is glorified, treated as if it were a virtue, celebrated as it were, we create a double standard. Violence does not respect the rights of others, or individual freedom. As a society, this puts us at cross-purpose with our own values. No group, political, religious or social, has the corner on America's values. Anyone from any sector of society who advocates violence is at cross-purpose with the traditional values of our nation.

A major change has occurred for many of us in recovery who have begun to live with real values instead of phoney ones. A significant number of gay men and lesbians have come to acknowledge how disloyal we have been to ourselves, how the denial of our feelings and the choosing of victimhood is no longer acceptable. I consider myself fortunate in living to see the emergence of a healthy sense of self-esteem in the lives of many gay men and lesbians. Along with this, there can be no question that the rules for survival have changed. It is no longer in secrecy that our safety is insured, but only in revealing ourselves in the roll-call wherever we show up.

Using this as a model for introducing change throughout society, we can begin by taking action which reflects the value we place on human dignity, on the freedom to live without fear of violence, and on the respect and acceptance of diversity which lies at the heart of the greatness that is this country.

MISSION IMPOSSIBLE?

Our task at this time is to stop taking the politics of hatred and violence for granted. We have arrived at the stage in which we must take the initiative for designing strategies in schools, churches, business, the military, and government to change the status quo. With the help of others, we can explore these strategies first in small groups, and then with larger ones. Gay men and lesbians in Colorado have become pro-active in reaching out in their communities to educate the electorate about the harm and hatred intended by the legislation recently passed in that state. The same education process is also taking place in Oregon, and it needs to go on throughout America.

We need to take action everywhere in order for society to begin to recover from its addiction to violence and hatred that feeds on shame and guilt. If we stop teaching hatred and begin to teach people about their own diversity, they can stop being afraid and angry about the diversity in others. Being a man, being a woman, will grow to mean being the person we are instead of the stereotypes which none of us are! Being advocates for health and recovery is the role I see for gays and lesbians at this moment in history.

Last May, as I returned from a meeting with others in recovery, I was mugged by three young men who were roaming the streets for all the destruction and outrage they could create. I fought back with every ounce of strength I had, and I shouted and called out for help as loud as I could while they punched and kicked me all over the sidewalk. The Guardian Angels, a street group united to put down crime in San Francisco, came to my defense. A woman no taller than 5'2" stepped out of her car to help me; people in the neighborhood rushed to my aid, and the police arrived with an ambulance ten minutes later. Covered in blood, no one asked whether I was gay or straight. They were responding to violence in their community. They were taking action against a common cause.

What I learned from this assault on my life was that had I kept silent, I might now be dead. For society to learn and understand how violence threatens the lives of all Americans each day, gay men and lesbians need to step out of the shadows of anonymity in which some of us think we are safe. Hatred and violence leaves *none* of us safe. When more and more gay men and lesbians show up and speak out, more and more straight people will acknowledge the message we bring. It is essential that we ask for what we need–what everyone needs: an end to lies, bigotry, and hatred and violence in our families, in our schools, communities, churches, government! By taking this kind of action, the process of bringing light where there is now darkness at the heart of homophobia will go forward.

There are and have always been men and women who are homosexual in our society. These men and women are our own brothers, our sisters, our mothers, our fathers, aunts, uncles, cousins, neighbors–they are our children! Acknowledging this will end the harm and introduce the harmony that can make all of us whole. From it will flow the health and well-being of our country in the 21st Century, and in it, the great diversity of all people can be encouraged instead of wasted.

The task is waiting for us, if we accept it. We have much work to do.

REFERENCES

Berger, R.M. & Kelly, J.J. (1994). Gay men. *Encyclopedia of Social Work* (Nineteenth Edition). Washington, DC: National Association of Social Workers.

Finnegan, D.G., & McNally, E.B. (1987). *Dual identities*. Center City, MN: Hazelden.

Gay Council on Drinking Behavior (1982). *The way back: The stories of gay and lesbian alcoholics*. San Francisco: Whitman Walker Clinic.

Heyward, C. (1992). Healing addiction and homophobia. *Journal of Chemical Dependency Treatment, 5* (1).

Kominars, S.B. (1989). *Accepting ourselves*. San Francisco: Harper Collins.

Kus, R.J. (1988). Alcoholism and non-acceptance of gay self. *Journal of Homosexuality, 15* (1-2), 25-41.

Kus, R.J. (1990). *Gay men of Alcoholics Anonymous: First-hand accounts*. North Liberty, IA: WinterStar Press.

Morganthau, T., Waller, D., Glick, D., Miller, M., & Barry, J. (1993, February 1). Gays and the military. *Newsweek*, p. 54.

Tuller, D. (1993, February 18). Gays fight image as sexual predators. *San Francisco Chronicle*, p. 1 and following.

Dysfunctional Relationship Patterns: Positive Changes for Gay and Lesbian People

Cheryl Hetherington

SUMMARY. Just as people who grow up in dysfunctional families often have some special relationship problems, so too do chemically dependent people and their significant others. Gay and lesbian couples are no exception. This article discusses some of the issues of boundary confusion, perfectionism, intimacy, impression management, rescuing and others to show how these patterns contribute to chaos and pain in relationships. Suggestions are offered to help gay and lesbian clients deal with self-esteem, boundary problems, and anger so that they can lead more balanced lives that include positive relationships.

Dysfunctional patterns of belief, learned behaviors, and habitual feelings make life painful. Relationships afflicted with chemical dependency in one or both partners are virtually always characterized by such dysfunctional patterns. Others may see a "together,"

Cheryl Hetherington, PhD, Founder of Hetherington & Associates in Iowa City, IA, is a psychologist, training consultant and writer in private practice as well as Adjunct Professor at The University of Iowa. Dr. Hetherington is the author of *Bringing your self to life: Changing co-dependent patterns* and *Working with groups from dysfunctional families: Structured exercises to promote health.*

Address correspondence to Hetherington & Associates, 123 N. Linn, Suite 2D, Iowa City, IA 52245 USA.

[Haworth co-indexing entry note]: "Dysfunctional Relationship Patterns: Positive Changes for Gay and Lesbian People." Hetherington, Cheryl. Co-published simultaneously in *Journal of Gay & Lesbian Social Services* (The Haworth Press, Inc.) Vol. 2, No. 1, 1995, pp. 41-55: and: *Addiction and Recovery in Gay and Lesbian Persons* (ed: Robert J. Kus) The Haworth Press, Inc., 1995, pp. 41-55. Multiple copies of this article/chapter may be purchased from The Haworth Document Delivery Center [1-800-3-HA-WORTH; 9:00 a.m. - 5:00 p.m. (EST)].

successful image, but the "real" person inside is insecure, feels like a failure and can be dangerously self-neglectful or even self-destructive. This dysfunctional way of coping with life makes people more dependent on things outside themselves than they have to be. A person may spend so much time managing and controlling work and relationships, that he or she has little time left for personal needs. This article is designed to help professionals understand the signs and symptoms of dysfunctional patterns in any individual and to explore the special problems and stresses experienced by gay and lesbian people. Methods to help decrease the dysfunctional patterns within gay and lesbian relationships will be addressed.

According to Hetherington (1989) there is a continuum of dysfunctional behaviors. At the less serious end, there is a contradiction between feelings and behavior. There are feelings of hurt, sadness and fear, and the mildly dysfunctional person will make excuses for or deny anything is wrong. For example, a woman may make excuses for her partner by saying to a friend, "She has been very busy lately. I am sure she will be very sorry that she missed your birthday party." Another person may be a compulsive cleaner and keep his home spotless. The busyness is a way to avoid the fear of facing painful feelings. While he looks organized and neat on the outside, on the inside he may be scared and feel confused or angry much of the time. Another person's thoughts and feelings may be unorganized and seem like a mass of confusion. Others live in a world of denial where they tell themselves that things really aren't so bad even though they are being abused. People learn not to feel what they cannot tolerate and thus become numb to their feelings.

In extreme cases of dysfunction there is shame, depression and emptiness. People feel that they have nothing to live for, and they feel hopeless and helpless to change. They think that relationships are something to hold on to by doing anything to keep a lover, and they will do anything to avoid abandonment. Symptoms may include suicide attempts, general depression, or chronic physical illness.

LEARNING DYSFUNCTIONAL PATTERNS

People start to learn dysfunctional patterns as children. It is a method of adaptation to, or imitation of, their family's style of interaction. Satir (1967) believes that dysfunctional families do not permit individuality, and members fail to develop a sense of self-worth. Dysfunctional families often create highly stressful, unpredictable environments, with many family secrets and rules that prohibit open communication. Members are frequently blamed, compared negatively to others, or called names. For example, a mother may say to her son, "You're just like your stupid father; you don't do anything I tell you." When children hear these messages from their parents, they internalize them, thus learning inappropriate responsibility and low self-esteem.

A parent may expect a child to assume tasks and responsibilities beyond their maturity level. For example, a 6-year-old is expected to call the parent's employer when the parent is too sick to go to work. Then the child becomes the parent and acts as caretaker for his or her parents. Jake, a 32-year-old gay man, says that he loved being in school and hated the weekends, because he and his sister were expected to stay in the house all day every Saturday during his childhood. From age 6, they each had to clean the house–scrub floors, wash clothes, cook, and do all the other household tasks. If they did not do it to the parents' satisfaction, they would have to do it over with little or no assistance from their parents. His mother and father did not help with these tasks and would watch TV or sit outside during the summer. Jake and his sister became the caretakers for their parents. He continues to tip-toe around them, tells them very little about his life, and protects them from a great deal of anger he feels towards them. He expresses his anger through emotional blackmail. He trades money (charge accounts, new car) for not bringing up his anger, particularly about the incest perpetrated by his father. Jake's parents would rather pay him off than deal with the anger.

Dysfunctional patterns of living develop in families where there is alcoholism, incest, chronic physical or mental illness, or another form of chronic stress. However, no major or obvious family problems are necessary in order for dysfunctional behavior to exist. Most often, dysfunctional behavior is modeled by parents and grandparents, and this behavior is considered normal even though it creates pain and unhappiness. Dysfunctional families with problems and/or secrets, no matter the subtlety, create *dysfunctional adult children* and are very common.

Some of the most common dysfunctional family rules (Black, 1981) include the following:

1. It is not okay to talk about problems.
2. Feelings should not be expressed openly.
3. Communication should be indirect.
4. Be strong, be good, be right, be perfect, make us proud.
5. Don't be selfish.
6. Do as I say, not as I do.
7. It is not okay to play.
8. You must always look good.
9. Do not rock the boat.

These messages are carried into adulthood. Adults who still use childhood coping behaviors which cause more pain than alleviate it are commonly termed "adult children." Many of the characteristics of dysfunctional adult children are the same–using the term adult children highlights the origin of the problems (Friel and Friel, 1988).

SPECIAL PROBLEMS FOR GAY AND LESBIAN PEOPLE

Gay and lesbian people especially learn about secrets and hiding from themselves and others. Berzon (1988) says that:

> The majority of gay and lesbian people grew up with a terrible secret that affected practically everything you did . . . Most of us were very much alone with our secret. You couldn't go for help to the people you would usually turn to because you knew, somehow, that they wouldn't like what you had to tell them. So you developed your sense of who you were as sexual beings in a context of confusion and self-deprecation. (p. 17)

To survive in the chaos, a child must find methods to cope. If that child is also gay or lesbian in orientation, he or she must be even more attentive to the "constant vigilance, strategizing and deception" (Berzon, 1988, p. 10) that is required to hide the truth of their feelings or pain.

Gay and lesbian people know that rocking the boat has grave repercussions. Family secrets can be that Dad has a retarded brother somewhere, that sister had an abortion, that mother takes lots of prescription drugs, that the stepfather sexually molests teenage daughters, that Mom drinks and verbally abuses the family, that Dad has affairs, that Aunt Peggy is a lesbian, that brother Jim has AIDS, that father is depressed, or that Dad and brother had a big fight which sent brother off to die in Vietnam. The family goes through complicated and painful gyrations—moving, lying to physicians, ending friendships, over-working—to avoid "rocking the boat" and facing the truth. *This rule, don't rock the boat, oversees and directs all the other rules in the family.* Some examples of how dysfunctional patterns appear in gay and lesbian people follow.

Excessive Concern with What Others Are Doing

By focusing on the "other" and how they behave, dress, eat, spend money, etc., one can avoid internal feelings and personal thoughts. How a woman feels about herself can be subject to the whims, moods or attention from her partner. Bev's partner may be sad and unhappy and Bev assumes that it is her fault and she should do something to make up for it, even though she does not know what is related to the sadness of her partner.

Public Image

Nice appearance is a treasured value in gay American male culture. Not only are gay men as a group concerned with fashion and style, they also tend to be very concerned with having fit and trim bodies (Etnyre, 1990). Like many heterosexual women, many gay men are perpetually "on a diet." If he is too consumed with the physical body and its decorations, the gay man may give too little time to working on his inner life. Continually worrying about weight gain and appearance may also lead the man to be unable to relax and enjoy such simple pleasures of life as good food.

Losing Contact with Their Own Needs, Goals and Feelings

Joan was in a managerial position at a university and had plans to go back to school to study in a specialty area. As she was collecting information about her options, she also fell in love with a woman who lived three hours away from her. Once Joan began to regularly see her new lover, she became confused about her goals and missed the deadlines to apply to the carefully selected programs. She began to talk of going to school in the town where her new lover lived even though the program there had little to offer in her specialty. This extensive accommodation for a three-month-old relationship nearly immobilized Joan, and she was unable to remember, let alone act on, her previous plan. She lost contact with some of her inner goals and wishes by focusing solely on moving to be with her new love.

Confusion Between Being Needed and Being Loved

Alice thought once that she could not leave a relationship because her partner, Nell, could not get along without her. Alice believed she had total control over and responsibility for Nell's well-being. Alice was confused about what love was: she was needed and therefore she was loved, and she thought that if she left Nell, that Nell would start taking drugs again and overdose. Alice later realized that the focus on her partner was a way to avoid the feelings and needs that she had inside. She had learned as a child that loving meant helping others and that her own needs were secondary. As an adult she did not recognize her own feelings (many of which were painful) because she had sought out others who were more than willing to accept all the care and attention they could get from her. Once she was able to become focused on her own needs and goals, Alice did not like or want to be in this kind of a relationship. She realized that being needed was not the same as being loved.

Trying to Be Perfect

It takes lots of energy to try to have a perfect house, job, lover, children, body, hair-do, political attitude or other symbol of being in control. When people try to control their environment so it appears that they are perfect, they are usually most concerned with what others will think of them. This is called "impression management." When people are highly invested in how others see them, in appearing perfect, they have little awareness of how they feel. Chris, a 23-year-old gay man, would race around the house to clean up when a friend called to say he was coming over. He hid the magazines under the couch, washed the TV screen, and cleaned the bathroom sink, so the house looked perfect. Then he would change his clothes so he would look perfect. All this in 10 minutes.

Social Isolation

People may have few intimate friends, and many acquaintances. People may have many friends who do not really know them, and with whom they share few important feelings. They do not let themselves be vulnerable with anyone. It is a lonely place to be when they don't call on others when they need to talk about being scared, sad or hurt. David is a very popular gay man with many acquaintances. He is handsome, in very good physical shape, funny and gregarious. He learned at age five to act responsible and mature. He does not show others his real feelings. He does most things in the extreme: He lifts weights to lose the weight he gains while binge eating. At age 35, he allowed memories of sexual abuse from his father to emerge. He is lonely, scared, isolated and says no one really knows him. He makes sure of that by making up stories about his life and lying about the smallest things. He is scared to let the feelings emerge from the memory. He believes that he will fall apart and his image of being "all together" will be tarnished. Since the memories are pushing to be remembered, he has started physically isolating himself more so that others will not see him fall apart. As David gets more aware of his frightening feelings, he increasingly isolates himself.

Fear of Being Alone and Fear of Losing Control

Tim, age 34, would do anything to avoid being alone. He worked long hours, then would stop on the way home to get a six-pack of beer for the evening. He stayed in the college town where he went to school and often dated younger college men. When asked what he liked about the man he was dating, Tim said, "He was someone to be with and he didn't mind having sex with me." Tim did not really like him; in fact, he thought he was rather immature and uninteresting, yet Tim would go to the local gay bar with him because Tim was afraid to be alone. Since this man thought Tim was all right, Tim continued to see him because he filled the scary empty spaces in his life. Alone, Tim might have to face his own feelings. Companionship and alcohol shift Tim's focus and responsibility away from himself. He became increasingly depressed and said, "I feel like my life has little meaning."

Fear of Intimacy

People often choose emotionally unavailable partners because they are afraid of emotional closeness, honesty and commitment. Sue was ending a five year relationship. She came from a home where the mother was controlling and wanted to know about everything that her children and husband did and said. The mother viewed any disagreement with her as a personal attack and would cry or pout and claim that no one appreciated her, and she was only trying to help. Most of the time Sue's mother was angry or complaining of a physical ailment. By the time Sue was a teenager, she was depressed, sullen and involved with drugs and alcohol. Although she had many friends and usually a boyfriend, she did not feel close to anyone. Her older sister was the family heroine, who made good grades, worked hard, did what was asked and appeared to have everything under control. At age 30, Sue lived with Lisa, who was a heavy marijuana smoker, did not work, had little education, but who knew how to have fun and laugh. While Sue demanded a neat and spotless house, Lisa brought laughter and some playfulness into Sue's life. Sue was also very possessive and jealous. Although Sue had fun with Lisa, they did not talk about their feelings and shared little intimacy. Although Sue felt obligated to take care of Lisa after a car accident, she did not feel emotionally safe with Lisa. They both smoked marijuana on a regular basis, and had little time together when they were not high. All behaviors were designed to avoid intimacy.

Fear of Abandonment and Unexpected Changes

When he first met his partner, Mark, Ed did not smoke marijuana. But as he joined Mark's group of friends who smoked dope while sitting around the kitchen table talking and laughing, Ed accommodated to this because he was afraid Mark and his friends wouldn't like him. He had learned this from the earlier childhood fears of being abandoned and had unconsciously accommodated because of these fears.

When people give up activities that they have enjoyed because a partner does not participate, they may become resentful and lose a sense of themselves as individual persons with important needs and interests separate from their partners. Because of Ed's fear of abandonment, he has never developed a clear sense of himself and grew increasingly unaware and inattentive to his own needs and interests. He abandoned himself for the relationship, whether with family, friends, or a lover.

Avoiding Conflict

People leave lovers, jobs, family, apartments and other important people and situations to avoid telling others about their anger. The fear of anger and rejection is so great that one's life can be spent running from place to place to avoid honest anger and conflict. A person may appear cheerful and always happy, yet have a steaming volcano underneath, full of unexpressed anger and disappointment. Beth teased and made jokes at staff meetings as soon as others began to disagree with what she was saying, and soon the topic was lost. Sometimes she would back down to avoid a confrontation for fear of someone disagreeing with her. When others disagreed with her, she perceived that they did not like her, and her co-workers' approval was more important to her than any of the ideas she presented. The avoidance of conflict goes along with the avoidance of intimacy and feelings of isolation.

Taking Life and Themselves Too Seriously

Marty was very serious, rarely smiled or laughed, and worked long hours to get more skilled at her profession. She would do anything for others, and always *seriously* wanted to know if there was something else she could do to help. When it was suggested that she needed to relax, have some fun, go dancing, or play a little, she solemnly responded, "I have been *working on* relaxing for several months now." For her, everything was work, and usually there was no time left to play. When there was, she worked very hard at enjoying herself. Her seriousness made spontaneous fun and playfulness difficult.

Excessive Concern with What Others Think, Want and Need

As "pleasers," they are usually very perceptive about what others need and will try to provide for these needs so that others will like them. Joel, a perceptive observer, is the first to pass the salt at the dinner table when someone simply looks up in a visual search for the salt shaker. Although he gets praise, attention, and appreciation, he is less aware of his own needs and thoughts. Some people become stubborn about knowing what others want without asking directly and set themselves up for rejection by forcing their "gifts" or "help" inappropriately.

Tolerance for Inappropriate Behavior from Others

Tilly worked hard on the night shift as a nurse in a hospital. At home she cleaned, cooked, did laundry and grocery shopping, paid the bills, and did anything else that needed to be done around the house. Tilly's partner, Jill, worked at odd jobs, spent much of her time at bars during the evening, and slept much of the day. She often took money out of their checking account to go buy lottery tickets or to go drinking. When confronted about it, Jill would tell Tilly that she used it to fix the car. Although she doubted it, she would say, "She needs to have some fun." For years she put up with lying, lots of hangovers, little personal attention and no financial assistance. Tilly tolerated these inappropriate behaviors for many years and explained to others that her partner was having a hard time and needed her support.

The Rescue Triangle

When someone is uncomfortable with others' distress, they feel compelled to try to fix the situation. Rhonda, a 35-year-old lesbian, worked in an agency that provided food service for a hotel. She was bright, funny and a hard worker. She was well-liked and had a lot of innovative ideas for improvement of the agency. Whenever other women in her work group complained about a problem, she was the first to offer a suggestion for change and tried to help take care of the problem. It was important to her to please other people, and she could do this by trying to fix things for others.

One day a co-worker, Paula, came to Rhonda and said, "I just don't know how I am going to get all the vendor orders completed in time to pick up my daughter from day care today." Rhonda said, "No problem, I will help you till you get them done." Paula was delighted, and Rhonda started working on the orders to *rescue* Paula. While Paula spent much of the rest of the day complaining to others about how much work she had to get done, Rhonda continued to work on the orders. When quitting time rolled around, Rhonda was still working on the orders and Paula quickly left, without a thank-you or an acknowledgement of Rhonda's help. Then Rhonda was steaming mad as she was left there with the orders still incomplete.

While Rhonda started out being a rescuer, she now felt like a *victim*. She felt that she was not appreciated and had been used by Paula. The rescue triangle was complete the next day when Rhonda started complaining to others about how lazy and unorganized Paula is at work. Rhonda had now become the *persecutor*. She expressed her anger and resentment by criticizing Paula who could not get her own work done, and who did not appreciate Rhonda's help enough to thank her properly. Rhonda, in her efforts to jump in to save Paula from her own responsibilities, participated in the "grand trio," the rescue-victim-persecutor triangle.

CHANGING DYSFUNCTIONAL PATTERNS OF LIVING

Lerner (1989) states that

> you can count on only two things that will never change. What will never change is the will to change and the fear of change. It is the will to change that motivates us to seek help. It is the fear of change that motivates us to resist the very help we seek. (p. 1)

Most people want to know how to change others in their lives and are less willing to take responsibility to make changes themselves. Yet this is what recovery is all about.

Because dysfunctional patterns are learned, they can be unlearned. Behaviors can be changed so life can be more satisfying and rewarding. People can transform the patterns they have learned. They can accept the gains and losses that come with taking charge of their life. Recovery from dysfunctional patterns requires life-long attention to the behavior targeted for change. Change can be a constant and rewarding avenue, and there are some specific ways to make these changes.

Gay and lesbian people with dysfunctional patterns need gentle, non-evasive care with a professional who can help them define their own boundaries of space and emotional closeness. In order to trust a helping professional, people must perceive none of the surprises and unpredictability they encountered with their families. The goals are to help them become more comfortable within themselves and within their relationships (Hetherington, 1990).

Learning healthy patterns is a long and arduous process. Interwoven into the dysfunctional emotional interactions, gay and lesbian people are exposed to the homophobia and stereotypes about lesbians and gays. They swallow this psychosocially toxic material, and it works against them from the inside. This increases the sense of shame, the need for secrets and the low self-esteem.

Hetherington (1990) suggests some general ways to help clients: (1) Believe whatever clients say and respect their boundaries. Although clients may not have a full picture of the results of their actions, it is important to accept their reality in the beginning. This is a start in helping clients develop greater identity and self-respect. (2) Encourage clients to keep a personal journal that is private and written to themselves in the future (five years from now). Gay and lesbian people from dysfunctional families have had tremendous practice at "impression management" (Hetherington, 1989, 1992). They have a public image of which they are always conscious. In a private journal, clients can collect data about themselves and observe their feelings and actions without worrying about the "unseen audience." (3) Encourage clients to use positive affirmations to curb high expectations. For example, if perfectionism is a problem, they can say to themselves several times each day, "I am okay the way I am" or "I did a good job." (4) Encourage clients to be playful and spontaneous. They may be good spectators, controlled and unwilling to participate in parallel play with others. A loosening of this rigidity can encourage inner awareness and expression. A sense of humor can be encouraged through modeling by the professional. (5) Explore the histories of relationships with clients. Although there may have been a habitual pattern of recurring relationships with addictive lovers, clients can begin to make other choices when they understand their relationship patterns. As they become more aware of their internal needs, they are better able to make healthy choices in relationships with friends and lovers.

There are some more specific problems to address. Some clients will not know where they end and another begins. This is a common boundary problem, and some feel it is the core of dysfunctional patterns (Beattie, 1987; Hetherington, 1989). People may take on another's feelings, responsibilities, or opinions—*confused boundaries.* Suggestions to help with confused boundaries include: (1) Taking a time-out. (2) Not committing to activities that will rescue the other. (3) When confused, focusing attention inside to know personal feelings. (4) Remembering, no one is ultimately responsible for another's feelings no matter how much others insist, "You are making me feel guilty." It is simply not true. People feel guilty because of their own interpretation and view of the situation. No one outside of another can control their feelings. (5) Setting and sticking to reasonable healthy limits or boundaries in all relationships. (6) Remembering that appropriate personal boundaries simplify life, rather than complicate life.

Many dysfunctional people may have not expressed *anger* openly and honestly for a very long time. Ideas from Beattie (1987) include the following: (1) Feel the emotion. Consider what the anger feels like in your body (breathing, tension, heart rate). (2) Look at the thought that goes with the emotion. See if there are recognizable patterns or repetitions of thought, like, "Someone is trying to trick me again." Saying such statements to self increases and creates anger. (3) Make a responsible decision about what action, if any, to take. Is it important to tell someone, write it down, or ask for clarification? (4) Don't let the anger be in control. Perhaps a time-out is needed to gain perspective. Some alone time to cry or scream may help. Time and perspective aids clients in knowing what they need. (5) Discuss anger openly and honestly when appropriate. Encourage clients to pick an appropriate time to talk to a lover about their anger, not when they are drunk, angry or tired. (6) Take responsibility for personal anger. Clients are responsible for their anger, not anyone else. (7) Burn off the anger energy. Physical exercise is often helpful to regain an emotional and physical balance. Walking, running, etc., are good. (8) Do not hit when angry. This is an unacceptable way to express anger. Clients can learn that anger is a feeling and that violence is an action. It is imperative to choose a different action (i.e., talking, writing, crying). (9) Write letters that will not be sent. As an effective way to discharge feelings without increasing guilt, clients can write out feelings to those with whom they are angry. It is also an effective way to discover personal needs.

Changing takes some consistent and persistent attention to *self awareness*. Gay and lesbian people who have some dysfunctional patterns have learned to be the way they are with many years of training and socialization to fit into the world. They have been encouraged to be like others, to not rock the boat. To change is a struggle that means paying attention to what they do, feel and say. It means that others will resist the changes. So it is up to each person to make the changes and to find supportive people and use the systems that will encourage personal changes.

REFERENCES

Beattie, M. (1987). *Codependent no more: How to stop controlling others and start caring for yourself*. New York: Harper and Row.

Berzon, B. (1988). *Permanent partners: Building gay and lesbian relationships that last*. New York: E. P. Dutton.

Black, C. (1981). *Repeat after me*. Denver: M.A.C. Printing and Publications.

Etnyre, W.S. (1990). Body image and gay American men. In R.J. Kus (Ed.), *Keys to caring: Assisting your gay and lesbian clients*. Boston: Alyson Publications, Inc.

Friel, J. & Friel, L. (1988). *Adult children: The secrets of dysfunctional families*. Deerfield Beach, FL: Health Communications, Inc.

Hetherington, C. (1989). *Bringing your self to life: Changing co-dependent patterns*. Iowa City, IA: Rudi Publishing.

Hetherington, C. (1990). The co-dependent client. In R. J. Kus (Ed.), *Keys to caring: Assisting your gay and lesbian clients.* (pp. 148-159). Boston: Alyson Publications, Inc.

Hetherington, C. (1992). *Working with groups from dysfunctional families: Structured exercises to promote health.* Duluth, MN: Whole Person Press.

Lerner, H. G. (1989). *Dance of intimacy: A woman's guide to courageous acts of change in key relationships.* New York: Harper and Row.

Satir, V. (1967). *Conjoint family therapy.* Palo Alto, CA: Science and Behavior Books.

Spirituality and the Gay Community

Father Leo Booth

SUMMARY. Father Leo Booth examines the need to recognize the effects negative religious messages about homosexuality have on gay and lesbian clients. He describes the difference between religion and spirituality, and offers suggestions for guiding gay clients into self-acceptance, even in the face of a religious and social environment which does not always promote such acceptance.

It's hard to have a healthy relationship with someone you believe does not like you. It's bad enough when the person you think doesn't like you is a family member, co-worker, schoolmate, or neighbor. It's worse when that someone is God. People of many faiths and ethnic backgrounds have suffered from religious persecution, but most of them had a faith or religion in which they could feel wanted and accepted. But gays are the only group who have been religiously condemned not for what they do, or what they believe, but for simply being who they are. Negative religious teachings about homosexuality have created a deeply embedded core of shame and self-loathing which surfaces in a host of dysfunctional attitudes and behaviors.

Father Leo Booth, MTh, CAC, CEDC, is a nationally acclaimed author, educator and trainer on spirituality and recovery from depression, addictions, and low self-esteem. Fr. Leo is a parish priest at St. George's Episcopal Church in Hawthorne, California. His latest book is *When God becomes a drug: Breaking the chains of religious addiction and abuse.*

Address correspondence to Spiritual Concepts, 2700 St. Louis Avenue, Long Beach, CA 90806 or call (310)-434-4813.

[Haworth co-indexing entry note]: "Spirituality and the Gay Community." Booth, Father Leo. Co-published simultaneously in *Journal of Gay & Lesbian Social Services* (The Haworth Press, Inc.) Vol. 2, No. 1, 1995, pp. 57-65: and: *Addiction and Recovery in Gay and Lesbian Persons* (ed: Robert J. Kus) The Haworth Press, Inc., 1995, pp. 57-65. Multiple copies of this article/chapter may be purchased from The Haworth Document Delivery Center [1-800-3-HAWORTH; 9:00 a.m. - 5:00 p.m. (EST)].

It is important to understand that religion and spirituality are not the same. Religion is a set of man-made teachings about God which often reflect social customs of the day. It employs rituals and doctrine which can either enhance spirituality, or damage it. Spirituality is God-given. It is positive creativity which involves choice, self-empowerment, and responsibility. Healthy spirituality requires self-esteem. It encompasses mental, emotional and physical well-being.

Unhealthy religious messages often damage spirituality. But for lesbians and gay men, shaming, negative religious messages about homosexuality can literally be soul-murdering. Most gays grow up unable to truly reveal themselves to their families and friends. This can make healthy intimacy extremely difficult for the over ten percent of the population who is gay. The deep-seated guilt, shame and fear which many gays feel manifest themselves in a variety of dysfunctions: low self-esteem, chronic depression, substance abuse, eating disorders, codependency and sexual addiction or sexual dysfunction. While these issues are not particular to gays, they present problems not found in the heterosexual community. Guiding gays and lesbians to self-acceptance in a society which tells them they are unacceptable requires keen awareness of and respect for the issues facing them.

I believe it is absolutely essential that all therapists, counselors, social workers and clergy be aware of these issues. Homosexuality is out of the closet and the days when a caregiving professional could spend years treating people without ever seeing a client who has some kind of issue with homosexuality are gone. Just the *fear* of being thought homosexual keeps people from revealing sexual problems or sexual abuse issues with therapists and clergy, even when that person is totally heterosexual. Ignorance of the issues facing gays does a great disservice to all clients, gay and straight.

In a treatment center where I was a consultant, a therapist was working with her group on learning to recognize how they project past relationships or experiences on current situations. In one such group, a young man was asked why he kept angrily avoiding a new woman patient who was extremely religious. "She hates me," he said. "I don't even know you!" the woman protested. "You don't have to know me to hate me," he said. "I'm gay." As he expected, the woman visibly recoiled. Unfortunately for gays and lesbians, their fears or perceptions of ostracism and abandonment are often grounded in all too painful reality. Certainly, gays and lesbians have their own issues with projection, but again, they are unique in being the object of religiously based hatred. I have watched similar scenarios in many treatment programs and therapy groups, and am still surprised at how many therapists do not know how to handle either religious addiction, or the inevitable conflicts which result from the collision of religious beliefs and homosexuality–whether between a gay patient and another's religious beliefs, or between a patient struggling to reconcile religious messages and sexual orientation issues.

When I counsel gays and lesbians, the most important work I do with them is to begin to identify all the messages they heard growing up about God, sex and homosexuality. I have found that identifying these beliefs from the outset provides valuable insights into addressing the many issues facing the gay community. In those messages can be found the seeds of the low self-esteem and self-destructiveness which sometimes appears far too prevalent in the gay community. Sometimes, these messages will actually drive gays into an extreme religiosity, often as an attempt to change or escape their homosexuality. Other times, it drives them totally away, not only from religion, but from a God they believe despises them, leaving them mired in a spiritual wasteland. Once you see how these messages affect them mentally, emotionally and physically, you can begin to guide them out of the shame and into self-acceptance.

I do not believe anyone can be spiritually healthy if they are abusing themselves mentally, emotionally or physically. To not be free to reveal oneself to another is one of the deepest abuses we humans can perpetrate on each other. Sadly, this lack of freedom often results in lifestyles, attitudes and behaviors which are harmful emotionally, mentally and physically. I do not believe we can truly know God if we cannot know ourselves, and let ourselves be known by others. Because of the overall social and religious prejudice against homosexuality, many people who, deep within themselves suspect or know that they are gay, hide this knowledge from themselves. Just recently I received a letter from a gay person who wrote, "I knew early in my childhood that I was gay, but I hid from it. I got married because it was acceptable, but the only way I could stand it was to drink and drink and drink." Others describe how they buried their sexuality beneath food addiction, workaholism or religion. Some have a long history of negativity, pessimism and outright rage at a world in which they are told they have no place.

So the first issue I address with gay patients is homophobia, both internalized and externalized. In my inservices, I teach therapists to look very carefully at any client or patient who is vocally anti-gay. That patient may well be harboring fears about his or her sexuality. In my book, *When God Becomes a Drug: Breaking the Chains of Religious Addiction and Abuse* (Putnam/Tarcher, 1992), I tell the story of Paul, whose fear of ostracism and punishment drove him into an almost violent homophobia, as well as religious addiction. Many people who have been sexually abused, or who have grown up unable to talk to anyone about their fears concerning their sexual feelings, often exhibit a vocal hatred and persecution of homosexuality. I know of no better example of this than Jeffrey Dahmer, the Milwaukee mass murderer of gay men. According to some reports I have read, he made a veiled attempt to discuss his sexual problems and seek help from a minister whose response seems to have only reinforced his own self-hatred and fear. I cannot tell you how many people I meet, both gay and straight, whose deeply embedded shame comes from having been told they are condemned or bad by someone who supposedly represents God.

I am often asked by therapists and social workers how to deal with this kind of religious-based shame. Even though I am an Episcopal priest with an active ministry, I do not engage in theological debate with people who come to me with scriptural texts which they think prove some point or theory. To do so is enabling the religiously addicted to engage in their "using" behaviors, or the religiously abused to continue their self-victimization. Instead, I work with them on such issues as the black-and-white thinking, inability to question authority, or need to be fixed and rescued which lies beneath the questions. I do not believe that any scriptural or inspirational text is written in stone. Times change; people change; social customs change. St. Paul exhorted slaves to be obedient to their masters, but today, slavery is socially unacceptable. I often point out that the Bible says "If your eye offends you, pluck it out," but I don't notice too many people cutting out their eyes when they've looked at something they think they shouldn't see. I always ask if we can abandon slavery and the "eye for an eye" brand of justice, why can't we abandon the teachings about women being secondary and same-sex sexual behavior being an abomination? Those teachings have no more place in today's society than the laws concerning slavery.

More important, rather than focus on what scripture does or does not say, I recommend examining whether that scripture empowers one to make choices, ask questions, take personal responsibility for the direction of their lives. For these are key elements of healthy spirituality. Gays and lesbians, like many other minorities, struggle with powerlessness and victimization. The prejudices are real. The spiritual devastation created by generations of clandestine, dual living is real. In both gays and lesbians, it frequently results in sexual addiction and codependency, or an "I'm going to hell anyway, so it doesn't matter" kind of irresponsibility. Gays and lesbians have tremendously complicated boundary issues in addition to very serious issues with intimacy.

When we treat gay and lesbian clients, we are treating a community which has been abused and violated on many, many levels. I believe a far greater percentage of the gay and lesbian population has been sexually abused than that of the straight community. This is in addition to the wholesale religious sexual abuse based solely on their sexual orientation. Because of the religious messages which teach that women are inferior or secondary, lesbians in particular suffer a double dose of injustice. One very closeted lesbian who is a teacher said angrily, "There's this double standard. Somehow, it's more OK for gay men to be teachers. We even had a man whom the staff knew was dying of AIDS, and everyone was very supportive—even the parents who figured it out. But I would be totally stripped of my career if I came out." While honoring that pain, it is necessary to move them out of the victim stance and into a spiritual empowerment which permits self-acceptance.

One problem I encounter is the extreme division in the homosexual community between the militantly "out" who want everyone out of the closet, and those who, in order to protect jobs and families, remain closeted or extremely guarded. In the heated exchanges between those two factions, I often see them duplicate the shaming and abusiveness they have experienced from the straight community. This is not exclusive to the gay community–I see it in many of the ethnic communities around Los Angeles. The important thing to understand is that the issue is not really about being "out" or "in," but the ability to accept difference, and to maintain identity and self-acceptance when others do not adhere to the same beliefs.

This makes the work with boundaries so very important. The reality is, not every gay person can be safely out. The rash of violence against gays which accompanied President Clinton's initial rush to lift the ban on gays in the military is proof of that. My experience with gay clients is that the person who so adamantly wants everyone out of the closet often does so because he or she does not feel acceptable and merely seeks validation in numbers. Yet, as the many sexual abuse survivors who have revealed their abuses can testify, there is great healing and safety in knowing you are not alone. Revealing something that another person does not wish to have revealed robs that person of choice and self-power. More importantly, it robs people of the opportunity to discover that their own sense of identity and power does not depend on the acceptance and approval of others. In victimizing others, people victimize themselves even more.

The issue of spiritual empowerment and choices is vital to healing the spiritual wounds of the gay community. So many choices which are routinely part of heterosexual life are much more difficult for the gay community. Yes, many straight couples struggle with the issue of whose family they visit during holidays and vacations, and how to deal with in-laws who may not get along. But when your partner is gay, and your family either does not accept the relationship, or doesn't even know you are gay, the issue takes on greater significance. I have been called on more and more, both as a priest and a counselor, to work with partners and families of gay and lesbian patients in the dispute over health care and estate planning when one partner is ill or injured. Because of the differences in laws governing or protecting gay relationships, the choices are sometimes limited. My focus is always in helping people see that, no matter what the situation, they do have choices, and they can utilize their spiritual power in working with the choices they do have.

By far, the greatest problem I see facing the gay community is the issue of creating healthy relationships. Gays and lesbians have no real role models on which to base healthy relationships, healthy lifestyles. I see them struggling to create happy lives according to the "straight" model, which I think is one reason there are so many dysfunctional gay relationships. For one thing, the heterosexual model is not terribly healthy to begin with, because of the gender abuse which casts the husbands as breadwinners and wives as homemakers and caretakers. So gays and lesbians are trying to create partnerships based on a model which more often reflects great inequality, control and submission.

Gay relationships *are* different. Just look at the issue of conceiving and raising children. For straight couples, the issue of children is often a choice based on economic and lifestyle situations. For gay couples who have not been married, the issue of children becomes a serious matter of the mechanics of conception, and the more basic issue of even being allowed to raise their own children. Again, that religious perception of gays being morally bad raises its head.

All of these issues bring great guilt, shame and fear. I have counseled many gays who married because they loved and wanted children. In some cases, their spouses knew at the outset what the situation was. Most of the time, the homosexuality was a secret, even from themselves. I watch gay men and women work hard to build good relationships with their children, only to suddenly find themselves rejected and abandoned when the children enter the peer-pressure cooker of adolescence. I know that some children of gays fear rejection or discrimination if they, too, are not gay. So much fear and shame to work through, and it all comes back to self-acceptance.

When I served as a consultant to a Gay and Lesbian Treatment Program, one issue I was asked about repeatedly was the issue of honesty as it relates to the Twelve Step programs. Many people believe that not revealing their sexual orientation is dishonest. They feel guilty that they are not "doing it right." Each person's situation is different. What I try to teach them is how to evaluate their circumstances. More important, the key is to shift from focusing on the areas which seem to demand dishonesty, and to focus instead on all the other aspects in which they can be honest and open. I tell people it is possible to be intimate and vulnerable with others without revealing all the details of their sex lives. So many people, both gay and straight, think sex and intimacy are the same, which is why many gays think they cannot be open and honest without revealing their sexual orientation.

Yes, to a great extent, this is true. But there is also a deeper honesty which goes with the healthy assessment of a situation. Choosing whom to tell about one's sexual orientation is another form of setting boundaries. It requires the peoplemaking skills which tell you whether this person can be safely entrusted with a very important part of yourself. I find that many people who are victims of any kind of abuse live in fear of all the wrong things, yet recklessly engage in a number of self-destructive activities. The task is in learning how to tell when you should genuinely be afraid. I call this "healthy fear," like the fear of running out of gas on a dark road which prompts me to stop for gas even when I'm in a big hurry. As I would counsel anyone who is working on trust issues, I encourage gays and lesbians to look at the role denial or defiance might play in their decision to reveal their sexuality. Are they setting themselves up to be rejected? Are they seeking approval? Do they remain closeted in order to gain approval? Does doing so fuel their sense of shame?

In the process of making the decision to reveal or not reveal their sexuality to others, gays and lesbians can come to a deeper awareness and appreciation of who they are. Codependency is rooted in abandonment of self, either by giving so much that there's nothing left, or in withholding out of shame and self-hatred. Choosing whom to reveal intimate information is one form of reclaiming personal power. It is a visible demonstration that people value who they are enough to share that specialness only with people who can treat them with respect. Then the process of coming out to another person shifts from a fearful or defiant "I dare you to like me/reject me" position to a more affirming "I have decided you are worthy of knowing who I am" stance which reflects self-acceptance and self-esteem.

Finally, I encourage all caregiving professionals: therapists, psychiatrists, nurses, medical doctors, educators and clergy to examine their own religious teachings about God. In the inservices I conduct at hospitals and treatment centers, I work with the staff on learning to identify how they may be carrying negative messages about God into their own lives, and projecting those beliefs onto their clients–both gay and straight. If you cannot identify and reframe your own beliefs, I do not believe you can teach your clients how to do it. If those messages have created any kind of homophobia, they will limit your ability to effectively counsel gay clients.

I also stress the importance of networking. I believe it is vital to be able to refer clients to support resources, or to professionals who specialize in certain areas. Especially when working with gay clients, it is critical to understand the links between sexual addiction, religious abuse and eating disorders. I once counseled a man who entered treatment along with his wife because they were having marital problems. Both were anorexic. He was also extremely religious. During therapy, he disclosed a pattern of sexually acting out with men near churches. Further therapy revealed that he had been sexually abused by a priest at an early age, and beneath that lay ritualized cult abuse. His religiosity and sex addiction derived in part from his attempts to atone both for his homosexuality and the early sexual abuses. Helping this patient required the staff to network with a number of professionals who understood how all his symptoms were related. Helping him would not have been possible had not the staff been trained to recognize all the symptomology: eating disorders, sexual addiction, religious addiction and ritual abuse. Equally important, they had compiled a list of resources so that they were able to direct him to a Catholic support group for gay men, as well as Twelve Step support groups for codependency, sex addiction and eating disorders.

So you don't necessarily have to be able to treat every issue your gay clients may present. You do need to know how to identify their issues and know where to direct them for help. This is particularly important for social workers, whose clients' needs span a wide variety of areas. Again, healthy spirituality encompasses mental, emotional and physical well-being. Therefore, I always encourage professionals to build a support network which includes physicians, chiropractors and body workers, educators, lawyers and legal aids, and clergy. Building a sound support network of caregivers from all disciplines is one way to help your gay clients reclaim their spiritual power and begin to heal.

Special Interest Groups in Alcoholics Anonymous: A Focus on Gay Men's Groups

Robert J. Kus

Mark A. Latcovich

SUMMARY. Millions of alcoholics around the world find their recovery in "working the program" of Alcoholics Anonymous (AA). Most AA members find belonging to an AA group and attending meetings to be very important parts of working the program. Many recovering alcoholics, however, find that "special interest groups" are highly desirable in their recovery. This is the case of many gay men who see gay groups as critical in their achieving and maintaining sobriety. In this article, we will explore the special interest groups in terms of their definitions, types, and history. We will then take one group, gay men, and see why they have formed special interest AA groups, the positives of such groups, and the limitations of such groups. Clinical implications will then be provided.

INTRODUCTION

Since its founding in June of 1935, Alcoholics Anonymous (AA) has spread throughout the world. By 1990, it had not only spread to

Robert J. Kus, RN, PhD, a nurse-sociologist who specializes in gay men's studies and alcohol studies, is currently studying to become a Roman Catholic priest. Fr. Mark A. Latcovich, MDiv, MA, is a Catholic priest in the Diocese of Cleveland, a faculty member at St. Mary Seminary, and a sociology doctoral student at Case Western Reserve University.

Address correspondence to Dr. Bob Kus, 28700 Euclid Avenue, Wickliffe, OH 44092-2527 USA.

[Haworth co-indexing entry note]: "Special Interest Groups in Alcoholics Anonymous: A Focus on Gay Men's Groups." Kus, Robert J., and Mark A. Latcovich. Co-published simultaneously in *Journal of Gay & Lesbian Social Services* (The Haworth Press, Inc.) Vol. 2, No. 1, 1995, pp. 67-82; and: *Addiction and Recovery in Gay and Lesbian Persons* (ed: Robert J. Kus) The Haworth Press, Inc., 1995, pp. 67-82. Multiple copies of this article/chapter may be purchased from The Haworth Document Delivery Center [1-800-3-HAWORTH; 9:00 a.m. - 5:00 p.m. (EST)].

over 150 nations, but many other groups had been born and patterned themselves after AA's 12-Step model of spirituality, groups such as Narcotics Anonymous, Overeaters Anonymous, Gamblers Anonymous, Al-Anon, and a host of others.

The 24-hour-a-day way of life of AA is a spiritual one. Living this way of life is known to members as "working the program" (Kus, 1988a). Activity clusters which encompass "working the program" are seven: (1) working the 12 Steps of AA; (2) attending AA meetings; (3) reading literature for self-help and personal growth (bibliotherapy); (4) sharing self with others; (5) recalling and applying common AA slogans to everyday life; (6) doing non-AA activities arising from living AA; and (7) doing everyday tasks as well as one can.

Many persons confuse attending AA meetings with "being in AA." Although attending meetings is seen as important by most AA members, it is only one part of "working the program." In fact, attending AA meetings is *not* a requirement for membership in AA; the only requirement for membership is "a desire to stop drinking" (AA, 1952, 1953, 1981). So, if a person attends a 1-hour AA meeting, he or she still has 23/24 of the AA program to live that day.

Because attending meetings is seen as so important, a variety of different types of meetings and groups have been formed to meet the needs of the millions of AA members. One type of group which has emerged is known as the special interest group, a group designed for AA members with some other characteristic in common besides alcoholism. Many AA members are quite opposed to such groups (Norris, 1989). Some believe that special interest groups are divisive and cause fragmentation in AA, while others believe regular groups (those welcoming all AA members) should be sufficient to meet the needs of all AA members. Others feel that the existence of special interest groups implies that regular AA members are closed-minded, intolerant, etc. Other AA members feel that special interest groups violate the Third Tradition of AA: "The only requirement for membership is a desire to stop drinking." As we saw earlier, however, attending AA meetings is not a requirement for membership, so having special interest groups cannot be truly seen as violating Tradition 3. Finally, many in AA feel that individuals attending special interest groups may put too much emphasis on their non-alcoholic specialness and not enough on their alcoholic recovery. While this could indeed happen, it would be a quality of the members, not a quality of the type of group they attended.

While many have condemned the special interest group, however, many in AA feel that such groups are very important for their full recovery.

PURPOSE

The purpose of this article is to explore "special interest" groups in AA in terms of their definition, types, historical background within AA, positive aspects for their members, limitations, and clinical implications. Instead of discussing special interest groups globally, we will explore one type of special interest group in depth, gay men's groups.

DEFINITION AND TYPES
OF SPECIAL INTEREST GROUPS

Special interest groups, or what Kurtz (1979) calls "special groups" or "special purpose groups," are AA groups which limit their membership to AA members who share another unchosen human quality (e.g., gender or sexual orientation) or a chosen human quality (e.g., a particular occupation). Although this article focuses on the role of the special interest group in AA, it must be noted that all 12-step groups, which are modeled after AA, also have special interest groups.

The most common types of special interest groups in AA are those based on gender (men's groups and women's groups); non-heterosexual sexual orientations (gay, lesbian, or gay-lesbian groups); legal status (e.g., groups designed for persons in jail or prison); mental health status (e.g., groups for AA members who suffer from some form of mental-emotional illness); physical illness status (e.g., groups limited to persons with HIV disease); in-patient treatment status; amount of sobriety (e.g., groups for newcomers in AA or ones for persons with 10 or more years of continuous sobriety); age (e.g., youth groups); or occupation (e.g., groups for priests or police or judges).

HISTORICAL BACKGROUND
OF SPECIAL INTEREST GROUPS IN AA

Many persons who argue against the existence of special interest groups in AA are unaware of the historical background of the development of such groups.

As early as 1945, AA co-founder Bill Wilson realized that often gay and bisexual men of AA were having more difficulty maintaining sobriety than their heterosexual brothers. At a lunch with a gay man named Barry L., Bill expressed his wonderment if maybe there should not be special gay men's groups in AA. When Bill asked Barry how much sobriety he had achieved, Barry answered "11 months." Bill told Barry to come back when he had 18 months, and they would discuss founding groups for gay men. Unfortunately, Barry never returned for this meeting, so gay groups were not formed until many years later (L., 1985).

Also in AA's history, AA was faced not only with accepting openly gay men, but also black members. AA groups began setting all kinds of "membership requirements" to join AA. When all of these rules were collected, many in AA realized that if all were followed, AA would have practically no members. The debate over who could join AA was basically ended by AA co-founder Dr. Bob Smith who said, "What would the Master [Jesus] do in a situation like this? A man is a member of AA if HE says so, not if WE say so" (L., 1985). Thus, the Third Tradition of the Twelve Traditions of AA was formed: "The only requirement for membership in AA is a desire to stop drinking." Thus, gay men and African-Americans were welcome, at least on a theoretical level.

THE PERCEIVED NEED FOR SPECIAL
GAY MEN'S AA GROUPS

Despite the fact that Tradition Three theoretically ended discrimination in membership, many gay men felt they did indeed need to have special groups in addition to participating in regular groups. They felt this way for several reasons.

First, many felt homonegativity (anti-gay attitudes) being directed towards them in regular AA groups. For example, many groups felt it was quite appropriate for recovering persons to talk about their opposite-sex spouses in their in-meeting sharing, but that it was inappropriate for gay men to talk about their lovers in the same meetings.

Second, some gay men felt that while it is indeed true that nobody is "terminally unique" as AA preaches, there are indeed important and valid differences between gay men and others which needed to be dealt with, rather than ignored (Bittle, 1982).

Third, as Finnegan and McNally (1987) point out, gay recovering alcoholic men have a dual identity which could lead to discrimination should it become public. Therefore, many men feel that their special anonymity needs as both gay and alcoholic can best be made in groups where only gay men meet.

Before looking at some of the positives of special interest groups which gay men have identified, it should be noted that attending gay men's groups is not viewed as either necessary or positive by all gay recovering alcoholic men. Some feel that regular groups are sufficient to meet their needs.

Other men feel that attending gay men's groups is important initially, but as the man becomes stronger in his gay identity, he may eventually become just as comfortable sharing his whole self in non-gay meetings. This idea is reflected in the following:

> . . . I'm not especially comfortable going to non-gay AA meetings yet. When I go I find myself feeling judgmental, bored, constrained, even threatened. It's mostly in my mind, I know. I wish I felt otherwise, and I believe my attitude will change. My beloved shrink said to me, "Most people tend to accept us in direct proportion to our acceptance of ourselves. All gays are homophobic to some degree." Once again, I can deal with the problems I have with "them" by dealing with my own attitudes. I hope to continue to grow and expect one day to feel free to share fully in a non-gay meeting. (Anonymous A, 1930, p. 133)

Also, it should be noted that attending gay men's groups is most often seen by gay men as an important *adjunct* to attending regular groups; attending gay groups is *in addition to*, rather than *instead of*, attending regular groups.

Finally, although many gay men have indicated in previous research that they prefer attending gay men's groups, many have to settle for attending gay-lesbian groups as gay men's groups are unavailable in their area.

POSITIVES OF SPECIAL INTEREST GROUPS FOR GAY MEN

Having seen why some gay men feel the need for special groups of their own in AA, we now look at some of the positives these men have identified from participating in gay men's groups.

One, it is often easier to establish trust in a gay group. When the wonderment of whether or not members of a group will reject one for his gay orientation is not present, the man can be more fully open and honest in his sharing, and sharing of self is a major characteristic of "working the program." As Jourard (1971) so wisely noted, self-disclosure is essential for good mental, physical, and spiritual health.

Two, it is often easier to talk in groups of persons who share one's own special life journey. As Crawford (1990) noted, the comfort level is usually far greater for many gay men in gay groups than it is in "straight" [sic] groups. [Actually, there are no such things as "straight" or "heterosexual" groups to these authors' knowledge; regular groups are open to all persons–gay, heterosexual, bisexual, and lesbian.] In a gay men's group, the gay man does not have to continually teach non-gay group members about such basic gay life processes as coming out or to dispel many common myths others may have about gay men, myths such as gays "choose" to be gay. As Goffman (1963) noted, being a "fellow traveller" is one of the reasons AA works so well as it does. In gay men's groups, members can share issues relevant to them as gays and as men, issues which can never be fully appreciated by heterosexuals, bisexuals, and women.

Three, the gay man can work on reducing his internalized homophobia in gay men's groups. Internalized homophobia, or not seeing one's homosexuality as a positive quality, is almost universally found in drinking alcoholics and in early recovery (Kus, 1988b). If the gay man cannot overcome his internalized homophobia and come to see his homosexuality as a positive aspect of himself, sobriety will be extremely difficult to maintain over time, and serenity will be virtually impossible. Gay men's groups can help gay men in this regard.

Four, attending gay men's groups can help the man build a new support system. In early recovery, gay men find their heavy drinking "friends" were not friends at all, but rather drinking buddies who would rather not be around a newly sober person. Because the newly sober gay man loses these "friends," and because he is encouraged to avoid gay bars, gay groups are an ideal place to begin building a new gay support system, a system which will not only support the man as a friend, but also support his sobriety (Kus, 1991).

Five, gay men's groups may help the man adapt AA philosophy to his gay experience. For example, in a gay group, the man may hear that internalized homophobia is something other gay men identify as a negative aspect of themselves while doing a Fourth Step (making a moral inventory). Heterosexual persons would never do this, as internalized homophobia is unique to gay and lesbian persons. He may then hear these same gay men talk about how in the Sixth and Seventh Steps, they become ready to have God remove the shortcoming of internalized homophobia and then ask God to remove this burden. Likewise, gay men may learn to distinguish what cannot be changed from what can be changed: while alcoholism and homosexuality cannot be changed, one can stop drinking and one can get over internalized homophobia.

Six, many gay men who have forgotten or abandoned God because of anti-gay bigotry hurled at them by traditionalist homonegative religious leaders come to find God in gay groups (Kus, 1992). Seeing their gay alcoholic brothers holding hands saying the Lord's Prayer, hearing the men talk about how God is manifesting Godself in their lives, and how they are able to finally thank God for the gift of homosexuality all help the gay man to discover or rediscover God. This function of gay groups is seen in this account:

. . . One evening I stood in a circle of gay men, including a Roman Catholic priest, and listened to the priest say, "Whenever any two or three of you are gathered in my name, I'll be there." It was a Mass in the home of a man I'd met at a bath house. I attended the service not out of any religious sentiment, but only out of a sense of social obligation. However, those words suddenly filled me with relief and joy. I felt a loving God in the room. I felt the same presence later, at my first AA meeting. God, the loving protector, had come into my life. And I have since come to see it was only my willingness that was necessary to perceive it. He had been there all along. (Anonymous A, 1930, p. 131)

Eight, attending gay men's groups frequently helps the man grow in service work for fellow gay brothers and for AA as a whole. It is not uncommon to see gay men's groups produce more than their share of leadership in intergroup, district and regional AA structures, and such groups often provide the stimulus for gay men to help other gay alcoholics as is seen in this account:

I am very active in gay AA service work. I have started, or have helped start, numerous gay AA meetings in rural areas, and I've co-founded a service group whose purpose is to provide outreach and education in the gay and lesbian communities concerning alcoholism. I continually learn more about alcoholism and how it affects us as gays and lesbians. These insights I share through writing, speaking at meetings, lecturing, researching, sponsoring, conducting workshops and seminars, and serving on various round-up and service group committees. (Anonymous B, 1990, p. 72)

Nine, attending gay men's groups often also helps the man become more community-minded or socially aware of his responsibility to his non-alcoholic gay brothers and to others in general. For example, as the gay man grows in sobriety, his internalized homophobia usually decreases greatly. As he begins to develop a healthy gay identity, gay pride grows. As gay pride grows, the man often begins to expand his horizons and wonder, "What can I do not just for fellow alcoholics, but what can I do for other gay brothers and people in general?" This often leads him to volunteering in the gay community as an AIDS buddy, a gay crisis line staffer, or political assistant. Experience with doing good works for gay brothers often then leads him to helping others besides gay men.

Ten, gay groups help the man learn how to celebrate life to the fullest in all its realms: sexuality, leisure, work, school, friendships, spirituality, etc. This is seen in the following two accounts:

> Up until shortly after my first love experience, I had only been to regular AA meetings, so I began going to a gay AA group in January. This group gave me love, understanding, compassion and beginner's lessons in the gay, but sober, lifestyle. I owe much to the group for the person I am today. I love my life; it is enjoyable and challenging. I can dare to dream today realistic dreams that are becoming reality. My journey to sobriety has matured me. I know that life is to be experienced to its fullest. I also know now that almost everything takes work and time and that nothing will be handed over on a silver platter, not in business, in relationships, or in sobriety. I've learned that it's okay to make mistakes and that I've always got a chance at the good life, as long as I continue not to drink or to use drugs and as long as I continue to go to meetings of Alcoholics Anonymous. (Anonymous C, 1990, pp. 152-153)

And, from an Australian priest who was finally able to overcome his internalized homophobia and the resultant relapses by participating in gay men's AA groups in Chicago:

> I have life; I know love; I value freedom and experience its liberation. I can feel the energy that we call sexuality giving me life, responding to life, and bringing growth. I can feel pain and depression now without fear of falling apart. I can know painful memories and share pain and suffering among others, and still give thanks for each day of my life. I have a spirit that is shared by all people, but which I could not know until I accepted myself as a unique and good gift from God. The knowledge of who I am is the first gift that a loving God has given me. Through AA, and through gay men's struggles for freedom and life, I can know life itself. There is a unity that I

sometimes experience, a unity to the world of things, people, and places. It is a profound unity of all creation with its Creator. Sometimes I can experience this, but only when I value the first gift of the Creator–namely, myself. (Anonymous D, 1990, p. 55)

Finally, gay men's groups often help their members reduce the misandry (anti-male feelings) which virtually all men experience as a result of their socialization process. The current anti-male rhetoric and the popular "masculinization of evil" may be counteracted in all-men's groups. Just as gay men come to realize that anti-gay prejudice is wrong, has been internally hurtful, and must be overcome for one to achieve maximum physical, mental, and spiritual health, so too must anti-male prejudice be identified for what it is: another harmful form of bigotry which is an obstacle for holistic recovery.

LIMITATIONS OF GAY MEN'S GROUPS

Although the positives of gay men's groups are many, there are some limitations. As will be seen, these limitations are not properties of special interest groups. Rather, they are properties of the individual misuse of such groups.

First, because of the internalized homophobia they suffer early on in sobriety, many gay men initially dread going to a gay men's group. For these men, it is often easier to go to a regular group initially and develop a period of sobriety first, and then go to a gay group where they can work on developing a healthy gay identity. This is seen in the following account:

And then finally as the [regular, non-gay] group got to know me better, they said, "If you don't want to talk about those [gay] things here, why don't you go somewhere where you can talk about it, gay AA." So, that's when I did start going to gay AA. And I HATED it! Oh, I did. I hated gay AA, but I made myself go. I told myself that it would be good for me to go and that it was just like all these other things that I had experienced–the change and being frightened and it being painful and it being difficult. And yet, something inside me told me that it would be good for me, and my group and the people that I knew and trusted told me that it would be good for me. And so it was like taking medicine that doesn't taste good. I said, well, I'm going to commit to keep on going whether I like it or not. And now I really like it. But it took me awhile to get there. (Anonymous E, 1988b, p. 36)

Before going on, it should be noted that there is no such thing as "gay AA"; rather, there is only one AA, and that AA has some gay groups.

Second, if a gay man goes only to gay groups, he may find the homogeneity of the groups to be oppressive. This is especially true in small towns where there might be only one small gay group. Attending only gay groups, however, is not a limitation of special interest groups, but rather of the individual for not attending regular groups also.

Third, romantic entanglements may become a problem in a gay group. AA has long recognized that sexual involvements can jeopardize recovery, so it has recommended to the general membership that women should only have women sponsors and men only have men sponsors (AA, 1976). Most gay men in AA feel this is a good policy even for them, for while there would never be a danger of a sexual entanglement with a female sponsor, only a man can understand fully the burdens and life journey men must travel (Kus, 1986). In answering a question about whether gay groups in AA are "really serious, or is it just a big cruising game?," Hazelden responds:

Gay alcoholics attend these AA meetings for the same life-and-death reasons that other alcoholics go to theirs. Those who use meetings for cruising are endangering their own sobriety. (Hazelden, 1980, p. 11)

Fourth, by only attending gay men's groups, a man is denying himself the wisdom which comes from the life experiences of non-gay alcoholics–heterosexuals, lesbians, and bisexuals.

Fifth, by only attending gay men's groups, the man may come to focus too exclusively on his uniqueness. It is good to learn that all people share many life problems, and that they have some solutions for them. These solutions can best be learned by getting the widest variety of ideas possible.

Sixth, should a gay man stay only in gay men's groups, he is denying himself the opportunity to practice being "out" in a relatively safe environment. Many gay men report they have used their regular AA groups to self-disclose their gay identities, and these experiences have helped them immensely in becoming comfortable with this initially scary process.

Finally, by staying only in gay groups, gay men are missing golden opportunities to meet their gay liberation responsibilities in two ways. First, they are denying heterosexuals the opportunity to know openly gay men, and knowing openly gay men is one of the most effective ways of reducing homophobia in heterosexuals. Second, they are denying closeted gay men who attend regular meetings the opportunity to have positive gay alcoholic role models. One man talks about how he and his lover find attending regular meetings very rewarding.

> . . . We are the only gay male couple in the program in our area. Since there are only three gay meetings a week in Lansing, we have to reach out to all AA groups. In all of them–gay or straight [regular]–we act as if everyone already knows that we are a couple. It saves the hassle of having to explain. The freedom we have because of that decision is worth the small cost. Learning how to trust straight people was a big issue for me in the beginning. But, as I went to meetings, I learned and continue to learn that while the specific situations are different, the feelings that are there are really much the same. I really believe that most straight people in AA are ignorant of gay folk, rather than being bigoted. The only way that they can learn about us is if they see us in meetings and if we are involved in service. We can also help assure that tolerance is maintained in AA by being around to confront people when they try to talk negatively about gay people. There are five or six people I can think of in the meetings that I attend regularly who are dealing with sexuality issues. I can be there for them, too. Besides, I need all points of view on the steps and on how to work them . . . (Anonymous F, 1990, p. 117)

A SPECIAL NOTE ABOUT RURAL GAY MEN

Often gay men in rural areas do not have gay men's groups of AA to attend. These men may feel especially isolated. Some suggestions are offered here which have been found to be helpful for gay men in just such a situation.

One, rural gay men need to keep in mind the common AA saying, "It only takes two alcoholics and a coffee pot to start a new group." Actually, the coffee pot is optional!

Two, most gay men are within traveling distance of a gay meeting or a gay-lesbian meeting. Many rural gay men attend regular AA meetings in their rural communities on weekdays, and then attend gay meetings on weekend evenings in a distant city or college town.

Three, rural gay men do not need to have a gay men's AA group to achieve and maintain sobriety and also develop a healthy, positive gay identity. On the contrary. Many men use regular AA groups to achieve and maintain a solid sobriety, and then use non-alcoholic support systems to eliminate internalized homophobia and develop a healthy gay identity.

Four, rural gay men should take advantage of reading positive gay literature. Bibliotherapy, or using literature for self-help and personal growth, has been a lifesaver to gay men in both city and country (Kus, 1989). This literature may be of a general nature to help in overcoming internalized homophobia, or it may be specific to gay recovering alcoholics. Large gay bookstores, such as Lambda Rising (800-621-6969), will provide the gay man with a list of books and deliver them on request.

Five, isolated gay men may write to gay men's groups in cities to receive a gay recovering alcoholic brother as a pen pal. This strategy has been useful for other AA members who are "loner" members, folks who are in areas of the world where there is no AA group to attend. The latest *World Directory of Gay & Lesbian Meetings of Alcoholics Anonymous* may be obtained from IAC, P.O. Box 90, Washington, D.C. 20044 or by writing to Alcoholics Anonymous World Services, Box 459, Grand Central Station, New York, NY 10163 U.S.A.

Finally, rural gay men would do well to attend regular men's groups in their area to work on reducing anti-male feelings they may (and probably do) have. Developing a healthy gender pride is essential for a holistically healthy man, be he gay, bisexual, or heterosexual.

CLINICAL IMPLICATIONS

Members of the helping professions can be of help to the gay alcoholic man in several ways.

One, have a solid knowledge of AA.

Two, be informed as to where gay groups of AA are, when they meet, how to get in contact with them, etc.

Three, support clients who use such groups.

Four, support the foundation of such groups when possible. Often helping professionals know of several gay men who bemoan the lack of gay groups, but such men do not realize there are others with the same desire. With their permission, the helping professional may introduce gay alcoholics to each other for the purpose of starting gay men's groups.

Five, remember that initially gay men may be reluctant to attend gay groups because of fear of being known as gay or because of internalized homophobia. Respect such a gay man's wishes to initially attend only regular groups.

Six, know where to direct the man to obtain positive gay literature to supplement his gay AA experience. What bookstores in your area have a solid gay men's studies section?

Seven, encourage the man to attend regular men's groups to reduce misandry.

Eight, while encouraging gay men to attend gay men's groups, also encourage him to attend regular AA groups to get a well-rounded AA experience.

Finally, give the man positive strokes for his efforts.

CONCLUSION

In this article, we looked at special interest groups in AA. After defining such groups and listing some of the most common types, we turned to one specific type of special interest group, gay men's groups. We explored gay men's groups in terms of their historical background in AA, the perceived need for such groups which some gay men have, the positives of such groups, and some limitations of some members' use of such groups. Finally, after discussing the special needs of the rural gay man who does not have easy access to gay men's AA groups, we provided some clinical implications for helping professionals who work with gay recovering alcoholic men.

REFERENCES

Alcoholics Anonymous. (1952, 1953, & 1981). *Twelve steps and twelve traditions*. New York: AA World Services, Inc.

Alcoholics Anonymous. (1976). *Questions and answers on sponsorship*. New York: AA World Services, Inc.

Anonymous A. (1990). "You are my beloved." In R.J. Kus (Ed.), *Gay men of Alcoholics Anonymous: First-hand accounts* (pp. 129-133). North Liberty, IA: WinterStar Press.

Anonymous B. (1990). Someone else just like me. In R.J. Kus (Ed.), *Gay men of Alcoholics Anonymous: First-hand accounts* (pp. 67-74). North Liberty, IA: WinterStar Press.

Anonymous C. (1990). Coming out in sobriety. In R.J. Kus (Ed.), *Gay men of Alcoholics Anonymous: First-hand accounts* (pp. 145-153). North Liberty, IA: WinterStar Press.

Anonymous D. (1990). Priest from Down Under. In R.J. Kus (Ed.), *Gay men of Alcoholics Anonymous: First-hand accounts* (pp. 39-55). North Liberty, IA: WinterStar Press.

Anonymous E. (1988). Quote in Kus, R.J., Alcoholism and non-acceptance of gay self: The critical link, *Journal of Homosexuality, 15*(1-2), 36.

Anonymous F. (1990). I turned to the Steps. In R.J. Kus (Ed.), *Gay men of Alcoholics Anonymous: First-hand accounts* (pp. 109-118). North Liberty, IA: WinterStar Press.

Bittle, W.E. (1982). Alcoholics Anonymous and the gay alcoholic. *Journal of Homosexuality, 7*(4), 81-88.

Crawford, D. (1990). *Easing the ache: Gay men recovering from compulsive behaviors*. New York: Dutton.

Finnegan, D.G. & McNally, E.B. (1987). *Dual identities: Counseling chemically dependent gay men and lesbians*. Center City, MN: Hazelden.

Goffman, E. (1963). *Stigma: Notes on the management of spoiled identity*. Englewood Cliffs, NJ: Prentice-Hall.

Hazelden. (1980). *The homosexual alcoholic: AA's message of hope*. Center City, MN: Hazelden.

Jourard, S.M. (1971). *The transparent self* (Rev. ed.). New York: D. Van Nostrand Reinhold Co.

Kurtz, E. (1979). *Not God: A history of Alcoholics Anonymous.* Center City, MN: Hazelden.

Kus, R.J. (1986). *The Alcoholics Anonymous sponsor and gay American men.* Paper presented at the 32nd International Institute on the Prevention and Treatment of Alcoholism, Budapest, Hungary.

Kus, R.J. (1988a). Working the program: The Alcoholics Anonymous experience and gay American men. *Holistic Nursing Practice, 2*(4), 62-74.

Kus, R.J. (1988b). Alcoholism and non-acceptance of gay self: The critical link. *Journal of Homosexuality, 15*(1-2), 25-41.

Kus, R.J. (1989). Bibliotherapy and gay American men of Alcoholics Anonymous. *Journal of Gay and Lesbian Psychotherapy, 1*(2), 73-86.

Kus, R.J. (1991). Sobriety, friends, and gay men. *Archives of Psychiatric Nursing, 5*(3), 171-177.

Kus, R.J. (1992). Spirituality in everyday life: Experiences of gay men of Alcoholics Anonymous. *Journal of Chemical Dependency Treatment, 5*(1), 49-66.

L., Barry. (1985, July). *Historical perspective: Homosexual men and women in AA.* Paper presented at the International Alcoholics Anonymous Conference, Montreal, Quebec.

Norris, J.L. (1989, Nov.). Our primary purpose and the special purpose group. *AA Grapevine,* pp. 17-19.

The National Association of Lesbian and Gay Alcoholism Professionals (NALGAP): A Retrospective

Dana G. Finnegan
Emily B. McNally

SUMMARY. In this article, the co-founders of the National Association of Lesbian and Gay Alcoholism Professionals–NALGAP–discuss the reason the association was originally formed, the influence it has had in the larger field of health care of gay and lesbian Americans, and some challenges of the organization for the future.

In 1993, twenty-four years after Stonewall (the event marking the start of the lesbian and gay liberation movement), a President of the United States who acknowledges the existence of gays and who promised to enable "gays in the military" to be out safely took office. In some ways, President Clinton's stance has helped to create some better conditions for lesbians and gay men. Many have

---

Dana G. Finnegan, PhD, CAC, and Emily B. McNally, PhD, CAC, are Co-Founders of NALGAP who have done extensive work for gay and lesbian recovering persons. They are also Co-Founders and Directors of Discovery Counseling Centers in Milburn, NJ and New York City.

Address correspondence to Drs. Finnegan and McNally, 708 Greenwich Street, 6D, New York, NY 10014 USA.

[Haworth co-indexing entry note]: "The National Association of Lesbian and Gay Alcoholism Professionals (NALGAP): A Retrospective." Finnegan, Dana G., and Emily B. McNally. Co-published simultaneously in *Journal of Gay & Lesbian Social Services* (The Haworth Press, Inc.) Vol. 2, No. 1, 1995, pp. 83-90: and: *Addiction and Recovery in Gay and Lesbian Persons* (ed: Robert J. Kus) The Haworth Press, Inc., 1995, pp. 83-90. Multiple copies of this article/chapter may be purchased from The Haworth Document Delivery Center [1-800-3-HAWORTH; 9:00 a.m. - 5:00 p.m. (EST)].

become more visible and more vocal and have begun to wield some political clout. Lesbians and gay men have been featured on the covers of *Newsweek* and other magazines. Some lesbians and gay men have been appointed to significant positions in the federal government.

But such visibility and progress have met, also, with powerful resistance. The current battles and controversies set off in 1993 about "gays in the military" have cumulated in a destructive policy of "Don't ask, don't tell" as a way of soothing and resolving the panic, discomfort, and homophobia of those who are opposed to gays and lesbians having a voice or being visible in our society. The controversy over gays in the military has become a kind of emotional center and a representation of the struggle between oppressors of lesbians/gays and those who advocate freedom and safety for lesbians/gays. The struggle, however, is counteractional–the more visible and vocal the advocates become, the harder it is for closeted lesbians and gays to make their way safely in this society. Paradoxically, openness elicits denial, not only in those who are gay/lesbian and in those who would help them, but also in those who would silence them. "Don't ask, don't tell" is the perfect paradigm for both external and internalized homophobia.

Those of us who have been activists in the gay and lesbian health field, especially in the field of alcoholism and other drug addictions, know that the concept and consequences of "Don't ask, don't tell" lie at the heart of what we have been fighting against for many years. We have had to fight the battle on not one but two fronts. The gay and lesbian communities have long been in denial of alcoholism and drug addiction as problems. They have often not acknowledged its epidemic proportions and ignored the truths that alcoholism and drug abuse cripple and kill. And the alcoholism and drug addiction treatment fields have long been in denial of their own homophobia and resulting destructive behavior. Too often they have ignored and not dealt with the major issues of sexuality, sexual orientation, sexual identity and as a result have failed at times to give proper treatment.

In July of 1979, the National Association of Lesbian and Gay Alcoholism Professionals (NALGAP) was formed in order to fight these battles. The original charter stated NALGAP's three primary goals: (1) to advocate for good, non-homophobic treatment for lesbians and gays suffering from alcoholism and other drug addictions; (2) to educate gay and lesbian health professionals about alcoholism/addiction; and (3) to provide a support and communication network for gay/lesbian professionals and other interested people.

The fifteen years since then have been filled with set-backs and victories of many different kinds. In 1979 there was *no* organization to speak out to either the gay or lesbian communities or the gay/lesbian health field about addiction. And no one seemed to be addressing the rampant denial in both groups. In the fall of '79, NALGAP was welcomed as a new member of the National Gay Health Coalition (NGHC) which was the first step toward educating the gay/lesbian worlds. Such education was sorely needed. At the first Lesbian and Gay Rights March on Washington in 1979, the Coalition threw a party for its members and served *only* alcoholic beverages. At the National Lesbian and Gay Health Foundation (NLGHF) annual conference in 1980, one of the keynote speakers told a "drunk joke," at which, of course, most people laughed most heartily. The lack of consciousness exhibited at that conference marked the cultural attitudes prevalent in both the gay/lesbian health field and the larger communities. No speaker at that conference addressed the powerful belief that the most common and acceptable way to *be* gay or lesbian and to cope with one's oppression was to drink and/or drug. Most people were not examining the fact that the bars and the baths were the center of gay/lesbian life and that lesbians and gays drank and/or drugged to facilitate their social/sexual interactions or to medicate the pain of coming out (or not) or the pain of isolation or the pain of being lesbian or gay in a homophobic culture. Most lesbian and gay health professionals as well as most gays and lesbians in the culture itself were filled with denial. The use and abuse of alcohol and so-called "recreational drugs" were generally accepted as a normal part of the lifestyle, as a part of the way of life. And most people didn't seem to want to know any differently. Alcophobia (the irrational fear of alcoholism or alcoholics) had the same effects on the lesbian/gay communities as did homophobia on the larger society–"Don't ask, don't tell." Alcophobia and homophobia are mirror images of one another.

NALGAP's experiences at the 1981 NLGHF conference weren't much more encouraging. We had a booth to give out information. A few people stopped to talk and take handouts. But most either peered at us suspiciously, walked by without looking at us, laughed, or ignored us totally. NALGAP's table at the 1981 Gay Pride March in New York City drew much the same reactions.

Fortunately, NALGAP became an increasingly powerful and influential presence. NALGAP members submitted workshops on alcoholism/other drug addictions to NLGHF and presented at the conferences that followed. In the meantime, a cultural revolution of sober people was occurring. There was a growing sober presence in the gay and lesbian communities which synergized with NALGAP's activities. For example, by 1979 gay and lesbian meetings of Alcoholics Anonymous (AA) and Al-Anon were being organized and were on the increase. In addition, annual lesbian/gay AA/Al-Anon roundups began occurring in major cities in the United States and Canada. Recovering gay men and lesbians swelled the numbers of people advocating sobriety as a viable way of life within the lesbian and gay communities.

NALGAP's influence in the gay/lesbian health field as well as in the communities continued to grow. At the 1983 NLGHF conference, NALGAP received the Jane Addams-Howard Brown Award in recognition of its advocacy of lesbians and gay men affected by alcoholism and other drug addictions. Both organizations had come a long way in a very short period of time. In the eleven years since, NALGAP has held two national conferences of its own (in 1985 and 1986) and then joined forces with the NLGHF to hold a mini-conference within the larger NLGHF conference every year. The purpose is to provide a visible presence about addictions, to disseminate information, and to provide a central meeting place for gay and lesbian professionals in the addictions field.

Fighting the battle against alcophobia among gays and lesbians, especially those in the health professions, has been a major task for NALGAP. The other major task has been to fight against homophobia and a lack of knowledge about lesbians and gays amongst professionals in the alcoholism/addiction field. As soon as NALGAP was formed in July of 1979, members began presenting about gay/lesbian treatment issues and needs at national and regional conferences on alcoholism/drug abuse. The fight for visibility, for recognition, for good, affirmative treatment for chemically dependent lesbians and gay men had begun. The impetus for impassioned advocacy for gay/ lesbian clients came from the many phone calls, personal communications, and heart-rending letters NALGAP received, spelling out the cruelly homophobic treatment many lesbians and gays had to endure in order to get any treatment at all. In the ensuing years, NALGAP's advocacy efforts increased and expanded.

In 1980, the National Council on Alcoholism (NCA) included in its annual national conference a day and a half long track on gay/ lesbian chemical dependency treatment. NALGAP served as a co-sponsor of the track, a promoter of this venture, and a distributor of the resultant literature. This was the first time that any major conference had recognized and attempted to meet the need for information and dialogue about this subject. The response to the Call for Papers was impressive: alcoholism counselors, psychologists, psychiatrists, social workers who specialized in alcoholism treatment and who had some experience and interest in working with chemically dependent lesbians and gay men submitted papers. Until this time there had been only two or three anecdotal papers which addressed the problems faced by lesbians and gays seeking treatment. Ultimately, this conference produced fifteen or so papers which then formed the background of the literature on treating gay/lesbian alcoholics. The gay/lesbian track and these papers were the first major statement that there were specific treatment issues which the addiction treatment field needed to learn about.

In addition, at this NCA conference, NALGAP members met with the Executive Director of the National Institute of Alcohol Abuse and Alcoholism (NIAAA), John De Luca, and engaged in a dialogue about the possibilities of NIAAA's support of NALGAP's advocacy efforts. We then arranged for a meeting with the Director and his staff to take place a few months from then. At that later meeting, the Director stated he would try to get funding for NAL-GAP members to meet and share information and ideas. In addition, he agreed to consider including gays and lesbians among those listed as underserved populations. He also invited NALGAP to send a liaison person to the quarterly meetings held by NIAAA. Although these gains were short-lived because of Reagan's election, NAL-GAP was able to achieve some recognition for its advocacy efforts.

NALGAP was busy in other areas, too. In 1980, in response to NALGAP's requests, the Rutgers Summer School of Alcohol Studies (SSAS) granted NALGAP members the opportunity to present an eight-hour seminar on gay/lesbian chemical dependency treatment issues. In addition, NALGAP helped form a gay/lesbian caucus at the National Association of Alcoholism and Drug Abuse Counselors (NAADAC) conference, thus creating a presence which required people to take note of the existence of chemically dependent gays and lesbians and the need for better treatment for them. NALGAP also became very active in disseminating information in an attempt to educate those who worked with gays and lesbians but knew little about them. From a number of state alcoholism agencies we requested and received mailing lists of treatment facilities in these states. Thus, NALGAP was able to provide much helpful educational material and referral information as well.

By 1981, NALGAP had become a vital force in the alcoholism/addictions field. Members were presenting workshops, seminars, and papers geared to teaching other professionals how to provide better treatment to their lesbian and gay clients. In this year the Rutgers Summer School of Alcohol Studies formally recognized the need for educating professionals by adding a course on sexual identity and recovery to its curriculum. NALGAP members taught that course as a special interest seminar on treating gay/lesbian chemically dependent clients. Two years later, the SSAS added a general lecture which addressed this vital topic. These activities continue to the present day. In the meantime, other schools and conferences on alcoholism and drug abuse around the country were beginning to recognize the need for courses and trainings about treating chemical dependent lesbians and gays. These were usually taught by NALGAP members.

The year 1981 saw the publication of two firsts: the *NALGAP Facilities and Services Directory* (NALGAP, 1981) which listed lesbian/gay-sensitive treatment facilities and practitioners nationwide and the *NALGAP Bibliography* (Finnegan & McNally, 1981) which cited "fugitive literature" (unpublished papers) and published materials about gay/lesbian chemical dependency. Nowhere else was this material available; NALGAP provided both access to and published this material. In 1982, two NALGAP members, Tom Ziebold and John Mongeon, edited the first collection of articles written by gay/lesbian-affirming alcoholism professionals for mental health professionals about treating chemically dependent lesbians and gays (Ziebold & Mongeon, 1985). In 1987, three major NALGAP events occurred. NALGAP published the first annotated bibliography of literature on alcoholism and lesbians and gays (Berg, Finnegan, & McNally, 1987). The Rutgers University Center of Alcohol Studies library provided a permanent home for the NALGAP Collection of literature on treating chemically dependent gay men and lesbians. And two NALGAP members, Dana Finnegan and Emily McNally, published *Dual identities: Counseling chemically dependent gay men and lesbians* (Hazelden, 1987), the first book about this topic.

In the years since its inception in 1979, NALGAP's phone number has become a kind of "hot line" for treatment professionals seeking assistance in helping their clients, for lesbians and gay men all over the country seeking help as they struggle to get sober in the face of terrible homophobia, those seeking good and fair treatment and the location of "special interest" AA meetings, and lesbian and gay treatment professionals seeking support in the midst of homophobic attitudes surrounding them. In addition, NALGAP publishes a newsletter which serves as a part of the support and communication network.

Over these years, NALGAP became a major referral source, a disseminator of information, an educator. But most important of all, it became (and continues to be) the national voice of conscience that advocates for all those gay and lesbian people who have been injured by their alcoholism or other drug addiction and who have also been injured by homophobia. It is a powerful voice that urges treatment professionals to provide treatment geared to the needs and realities of lesbians and gay men. This voice calls for safety in the face of homophobia; for a recognition and respect for the tremendous diversity among people's sexual practices, orientation, and identity. This voice calls for a recognition and respect for the pain and difficulties faced by lesbians, gay men, bisexuals, and those confused about their sexual identity, especially as they are struggling to become clean and sober. This voice urges acknowledgement of the complexity of *every* person's life, acceptance of lesbians' and gay men's uniqueness as human beings. This voice calls forth the best that the alcoholism treatment field has to offer.

So, now, fourteen years after NALGAP was founded, where do things stand? Times are still very hard for gays and lesbians–indeed, in some ways they are harder. AIDS has swept through our ranks, and we have lost many of our powerful and important leaders. Treatment programs have been hard hit by the Reagan-Bush years and many have given up trying to train staff and tailor any of their programs to attend to those who are different. And homophobia seems to have become the reigning prejudice of the Nineties.

So, what now? Where do we go from here? Now, perhaps more than ever, there is a need for a strong, open, direct, honest voice. A voice that speaks out against the injustices, the cruelties, the destructiveness. A voice that argues that lesbians and gay men must be accorded fair and competent treatment. A voice that advocates for those not yet able to do so in their own behalf. That voice is NALGAP.

REFERENCES

Berg, S.L., Finnegan, D.G., & McNally, E.B. (1987). *The NALGAP annotated bibliography: Alcoholism, substance abuse, and lesbians/gay men.* Fort Wayne, IN: NALGAP.

Finnegan, D.G. and McNally, E.B. (1981). *NALGAP bibliography.* New York: NALGAP.

Finnegan, D.G. and McNally, E.B. (1987). *Dual identities: Counseling chemically dependent gay men and lesbians.* Center City, MN: Hazelden.

NALGAP (1981). *NALGAP facilities and services directory.* New York: NALGAP, 11-47 S. Alvarado Street, Los Angeles, CA 90006 (213-381-8524).

Ziebold, T.O. and Mongeon, J.E. (Eds.). (1985). *Gay and sober: Directions for counseling and therapy.* New York: Harrington Park Press, Inc. (First published as Vol. 7, No. 4, *Journal of Homosexuality.*)

Referrals and Resources
for Chemically Dependent
Gay and Lesbian Clients

Robert J. Kus
George Byron Smith

SUMMARY. Alcoholism and other forms of chemical dependency have the potential to cause havoc in all realms of life. Not surprisingly, then, recovering persons and their loved ones often need a myriad of resources. In addition to the resources which would likely be needed by any recovering persons, gay and lesbian persons often need resources specific to their needs as gays and lesbians. Many social workers and other helping professionals, however, do not know how to go about finding out what gay and lesbian resources are available to them, and therefore are unable to make needed referrals for such clients. The purpose of this article is to discuss some of the unique problems which gay and lesbian recovering persons and their loved ones may have which might necessitate referrals, how to decide whether one should treat or refer, some basic resources which may be available to helping professionals to meet these specific gay and/or lesbian needs, and how to go about finding out what is available in one's community.

Robert J. Kus, RN, PhD, a nurse-sociologist who specializes in gay men's studies and alcohol studies, is currently studying to become a Roman Catholic priest. Mr. Smith, RN, MSN, an award-winning author, is Nursing Quality Management Projects Coordinator at Memorial Hospital in Tampa, Florida.

Address correspondence to Dr. Bob Kus, 28700 Euclid Avenue, Wickliffe, OH 44092-2527 USA.

[Haworth co-indexing entry note]: "Referrals and Resources for Chemically Dependent Gay and Lesbian Clients." Kus, Robert J., and George Byron Smith. Co-published simultaneously in *Journal of Gay & Lesbian Social Services* (The Haworth Press, Inc.) Vol. 2, No. 1, 1995, pp. 91-107; and: *Addiction and Recovery in Gay and Lesbian Persons* (ed: Robert J. Kus) The Haworth Press, Inc., 1995, pp. 91-107. Multiple copies of this article/chapter may be purchased from The Haworth Document Delivery Center [1-800-3-HAWORTH; 9:00 a.m. - 5:00 p.m. (EST)].

BACKGROUND

Chronic conditions such as alcoholism and other forms of chemical dependency can negatively affect all realms of life for those afflicted and their loved ones, realms such as spirituality, mental health, physical health, leisure, legal status, family relations, sexuality, citizenship, friendship circles, job, school, finances, lover or spouse relationships, and others. It is not surprising, then, that social workers and other helping professionals frequently find that they must refer their chemically dependent clients to others for needed assistance with particular problems.

Like other chemically dependent persons, gays and lesbians may also need referrals. But unlike heterosexual persons, they often have special needs which call for special resources. Unfortunately, many social workers may be unfamiliar with the special needs of gay and/or lesbian clients. They may be undecided whether they should attempt to treat these special needs or to refer the client for specialized treatment. They often do not know what kinds of special resources are available to meet these special needs or even how to go about finding out what is available for gay and lesbian persons in their community. This is especially true in rural America where gay and lesbian resources are scarce and which, if they are available, are relatively hidden from the average social worker.

PURPOSE

The purpose of this article is to discuss referrals and resources specific to meeting the special needs which chemically dependent gay and lesbian clients may have. Specifically, this article looks at some of the special gay and lesbian issues which may need attention in addition to the problems common to all recovering persons and their loved ones, how social workers can decide whether they should treat the client themselves or whether they should refer, what resources are available to meeting the special needs of gay and lesbian persons, and how to go about finding out what and where these resources are in their own communities.

POSSIBLE SPECIAL TREATMENT NEEDS

In this section we explore some of the issues which are unique to gay and/or lesbian persons, which are found more prevalently in this population, or which have dimensions which may indicate special forms of treatment.

Internalized homophobia, a condition unique to gay and lesbian persons, is seeing one's homosexuality as a negative, rather than positive, aspect of one's self. This condition is basically universal in all gay and lesbian persons when they come to recognize their sexual orientation. In time, however, it can dissipate. For gay and lesbian alcoholics, internalized homophobia will not disappear until after sobriety is achieved and maintained through time (Kus, 1988). Unfortunately, many gay and lesbian alcoholics do not recognize their internalized homophobia because it is being masked with alcohol and other mind-altering drugs. Many report that it is not until they have been sober for a year or more that they recognize how much internalized homophobia they did have.

Some of the signs and symptoms of internalized homophobia include low self-esteem, chronic anxiety, inability to concentrate, treating other gay or lesbian persons poorly, passing as straight (although this does not always indicate internalized homophobia), physical illnesses, feelings of estrangement from God, continual striving for high achievement (one of the few nice symptoms), inability to engage in same-sex sexual activity without being anesthetized with alcohol or other mind-altering drugs, and even violence towards self.

Fortunately, internalized homophobia is treatable with sobriety, getting to know positive gay or lesbian people, praying for acceptance of the gift of homosexuality, and by reading positive gay or lesbian literature (Kus, 1987).

Chemical dependency treatment may have certain aspects unique to some gay and lesbian persons. Many feel, for example, that they prefer gay or lesbian meetings of Alcoholics Anonymous or other support groups for their recovery to be adequate. Others, however, do not have such feelings and believe that regular groups are sufficient to meet their recovery needs. Still others, racked with profound internalized homophobia or fear of harm from others, refuse to go to special support groups. [See the article by Kus and Latcovich on Special Interest Groups in AA in this collection.]

Some gays and lesbians may even feel they need special treatment programs designed just for gays and lesbians, just for women, or just for men. Some gays and lesbians, who have been treated in a less-than-kind way by organized religion, may reject AA because it talks about God. Such persons, who confuse spirituality (found in AA) with religion, may want to be referred to such groups as Secular Organizations for Sobriety (SOS) or other non-12-Step groups.

Social workers who do treat large numbers of chemically dependent gays and lesbians and/or their loved ones might consider building a reference library with literature specific to addressing the gay and/or lesbian chemically dependent person. A beginning collection might include such works as Crawford's *Easing the ache: Gay men recovering from compulsive behaviors* (1990); Finnegan and McNally's *Dual identities: Counseling chemically dependent gay men and lesbians* (1987); the Gay Council on Drinking Behavior's *The way back: The stories of gay and lesbian alcoholics* (1981, 1982); Kominars' *Accepting ourselves: The Twelve-Step journey of recovery from addictions for gay men and lesbians* (1989); Kus' *Gay men of Alcoholics Anonymous: First-hand accounts* (1990a); Weinstein's *Lesbians and gay men: Chemical dependency treatment issues* (1992); and Ziebold and Mongeon's *Gay and sober: Directions for counseling and therapy* (1982).

HIV disease, including AIDS, has afflicted gay men more than any other category of Americans, while it has afflicted lesbians the least of all major social categories. Among gay recovering alcoholic men, it is quite common to find many who are HIV-positive. Social workers need to know the basics about HIV disease, which includes AIDS. [See the article in this collection by Dr. Pohl]. Among the things social workers should know, in addition to the basic biology of AIDS, are such things as what is available in their communities for persons with AIDS (PWAs, not "AIDS victims"!), whether or not there is an AIDS Buddies program or similar support for PWAs, where to assist clients in getting help with medication and other health care expenses, where to get specific help for clients with HIV-related problems with finances, job security, school issues, relationship issues, sexuality issues, family relationships, legal issues, and the like. They also need to know the difference between "confidentiality" testing (not recommended) and "anonymity testing" (recommended) and where to get anonymity testing in their community. Hospice care may also be needed in the last days of one's AIDS, and respite care might be needed for the lover who is taking care of his or her dying loved one at home.

Gays and lesbians in recovery may also need special assistance with *relationship problems*. Not all couples counselors are qualified to treat gay/lesbian couples. While a couple is a couple is a couple on the one hand, gay and lesbian couples often have problems different from cosexual (male-female) couples. For example, is the presenting problem a relational one or is it the result of the two persons being in different stages of the coming-out process? What are the levels of internalized homophobia in each member? If one has relatively high internalized homophobia, and the other has very low internalized homophobia, the relationship will definitely have problems–problems not treatable with conventional couples counseling techniques. While the therapist does not need to be gay to treat gay couples, or lesbian to treat lesbian couples, s-he does need to be sensitive to the needs of gay and lesbian couples, know basic challenges which face gay and lesbian persons (coming-out, internalized homophobia, etc.), and have solid experience in this area.

Treating *mental health problems* may also be a little trickier for gay and lesbian clients. In most chemically dependent clients, depression and other forms of emotional disease fade away in sobriety. Sometimes, however, depression and other problems may turn out to be independent of the chemical dependency and need professional treatment. When this is the case in gay and lesbian clients, social workers need to be sure the therapist is not homonegative (anti-gay or anti-lesbian). Horror stories abound where a heterosexist therapist tries to "change" a gay or lesbian person into a heterosexual rather than treating, for example, internalized homophobia. Internalized homophobia can be, and should be, changed; homosexuality, like heterosexuality, cannot be changed. (Heterosexism is the belief system that heterosexuality is a superior gift compared to homosexuality.)

A competent helping professional will include the client's loved one in the plan of care if the client has a partner, and the competent professional will have a strong knowledge base in chemical dependency, as this is a condition which afflicts so many gay and lesbian Americans either directly or via relationships. Such a knowledge base is critical so that CD-related problems can be distinguished from non-CD-related ones.

A basic reference library which addresses the specific treatment needs of gays and lesbians would be a wise investment for any social worker. Such a collection might contain the following: Coleman's *Psychotherapy with homosexual men and women* (1988); Hall's *The lavender couch: A consumer's guide to psychotherapy for lesbians and gay men* (1985); Kus' *Keys to caring: Assisting your gay and lesbian clients* (1990b); Moses and Hawkins' *Counseling lesbian women and gay men: A life-issues approach* (1982); and Woodman and Lenna's *Counseling with gay men and lesbians* (1980).

Sometimes gay and lesbian addicts alienate their families while drinking and drugging, creating *family problems* which need special attention. Sometimes such clients deliberately reject their biological families, assuming, often incorrectly, that if their families knew of their sexual orientation that they would reject them. As they grow in sobriety, however, many gays and lesbians attempt to make amends to their biological families. Because a tremendous number of gay and lesbian Americans follow the 12-step way of life, and because this way of life stresses the importance of honesty, many recovering gays and lesbians self-disclose their sexual orientation to their families for the first time when sober. Usually this goes quite well. However, there are the occasional times when rejection occurs. In these cases, social workers may need to intervene if the client desires the additional outside help.

Social workers must also be aware of the *sexuality issues* with which chemically dependent gays and lesbians may be dealing. Social workers should be knowledgeable about the various levels of safety in sex, for example, safe sex (e.g., masturbation), safer but risky sex (e.g., penile-anal intercourse with the use of a condom or oral-vaginal sex with use of a dental dam), and unsafe sex (e.g., unprotected penile-anal sex). Helping professionals should also be aware that engaging in unsafe sex is quite often *not* the result of a "knowledge deficit" in the intoxicated person but, rather, is the result of the lack of inhibitions which accompanies intoxication. Sexual performance difficulties may be present before recovery, and gay and lesbian clients may need support in overcoming them. In early sobriety, gays and lesbians may feel awkward, just like their bisexual and heterosexual counterparts, having sex soberly. Without alcohol and other drugs to anesthetize internalized homophobia, many feel very strange having sex in early sobriety. They often need reassurance that this is a normal state of affairs and should eventually pass with continued sobriety.

HIV-positive clients may need additional assistance in the area of sexuality. How can they get their sexual desires met while protecting others? What are the various ethical-moral issues they must consider in informing their potential sexual partners?

Finally, it is not uncommon for chemically dependent gays and lesbians to have sexaholism which needs treatment. Because self-help groups for sexaholics have radically differing ideas of "sobriety" and what kinds of behaviors are allowable and not allowable, social workers should have a very clear idea about the differences between the various groups such as SA (Sexaholics Anonymous), SAA (Sex Addicts Anonymous), Compulsive Cruisers Anonymous, and others.

Chemically dependent gays and lesbians may have profound *spiritual needs* which can often be met in 12-Step groups. When one's behavior is out of sync with one's value system, a condition almost universal among the using addict/alcoholic, spiritual conflict arises. Such spiritual problems as a sense of meaninglessness, hopelessness, and feelings of worthlessness often need special attention.

Because many gays and lesbians have been treated in such a heterosexist, homonegative, and unloving manner by many clergy in organized religion, they often have very special and profound *religious needs* which social workers may need to refer. If clients' internalized homophobia, for example, seems particularly intractable, and if the basis for this is religious in nature, perhaps religious referrals may be necessary. However, social workers must never refer gays and lesbians to clergy without knowing the clergy to whom the referral is being made. How comfortable is the priest, minister, or rabbi with gays and lesbians? Are they gay or lesbian themselves? If so, how comfortable is the clergyperson with his or her own homosexuality? If s-he is suffering from a great deal of internalized homophobia, s-he will communicate this to the client and make matters worse! Likewise, the homonegative heterosexual clergyperson can also do much damage if s-he thrusts her or his homonegative feelings onto the client.

Leisure issues may also take on a special twist for gay and lesbian clients. In AA and other 12-step programs, persons are usually told to change their "playmates and playgrounds." Many gay and lesbian alcoholics use gay and/or lesbian bars as their primary leisure source. Such bars are not only sources of drinking, but they are one of the few places gays and lesbians have for making gay and lesbian friends, especially in small cities and rural communities. Such bars are also sources of social and political news important in the gay and lesbian communities, and they are places where one may meet his or her potential life mate. Many recovering gays and lesbians feel, therefore, that the admonishment to stay out of bars unless they have a good reason to go into them should not apply to them. Many recovering gays and lesbians eventually do return to such bars soberly by using various strategies to guard against slips. Social workers may find gay and recovering alcoholics who do go to bars may be ideal referral sources for gays and lesbians who wonder about returning to the bar scene. Many recovering persons, gay and non-gay alike, find a world full of fascinating leisure activities they never considered while drinking and drugging.

Some chemically dependent gay and lesbian persons find they have special *legal issues* which must be addressed. While consequences for drunk driving are the same for everyone, at least theoretically, chemical dependency may lead to divorce and custody battles which have a gay/lesbian slant. For example, many married gays and lesbians who divorce as a result of their drinking also may face loss of custody of their children simply because of their sexual orientation. If the person facing loss of custody is a gay man, he is doubly cursed in the legal system: he is gay and he is a man, both social categories which American courts have treated with contempt in family issues.

Clients who are *HIV-positive*, in addition to being chemically dependent, may need special legal help fighting discrimination from insurance companies, the workplace, and health care institutions. They may need help in making out wills and durable power-of-attorney documents so that their biological families will not be able to overturn their and their significant other's wishes.

Finally, many chemically dependent persons find that their *friendship circles* change radically in sobriety. Chemically dependent gay and lesbian persons used to finding their support system in bars are often fearful of sobriety as it is in bars where their "friends" are. In sobriety, however, they usually find that many of their so-called "friends" are not actually friends after all; rather, they are drinking buddies who abandon them as they sober up (Kus, 1991). When recovering gay and lesbian clients ask where they can go to make new friendship circles, social workers should have some answers. If they do not have concrete suggestions, they might consider referral.

Having explored some of the special issues which chemically dependent gay and lesbian persons have, we now turn to the issue of whether to treat or refer.

DECIDING WHETHER TO TREAT OR REFER

The purpose of this section is to help the social worker determine when to refer and when to treat. But before discussing this, it is important to note that it is often more important that the social worker show genuine concern for the client rather than to have all the answers. Helping professionals who communicate love and faith and hope and compassion are much more effective than a clinically sterile type of person who, though s-he may have a good knowledge base, communicates disdain, disinterest, or homonegativity.

Reasons to Refer

Social workers should refer when faced with several scenarios. First, they should refer when they are uncomfortable with the client. This discomfort could be from the client's sexual orientation, gender, specific presenting problem, or the like. No helping professional likes all clients. Wise professionals refer these clients to others if they feel they cannot give these clients their very best.

Second, they should refer if the client presents with problems outside their realm of expertise.

Third, social workers often refer the gay or lesbian client to support groups or therapists in the gay or lesbian community so the client can get hooked up with such communities for solid, long-term growth. Developing a healthy gay or lesbian pride is essential for maximum health–spiritual, mental, and physical–for all gay and lesbian persons. This can best be achieved in a supportive gay or lesbian community.

Fourth, social workers often refer gay and lesbian clients if they suspect the client may be more comfortable or open with persons in the gay or lesbian community.

Fifth, sometimes referrals to groups such as AA are necessary because they can provide a way of life which cannot be provided in a 1:1 setting.

Before referring gay and lesbian clients, however, social workers would do well to look for the following qualities in the referral agency–be it a person or group: (1) The referral agent should be knowledgeable about alcoholism and other forms of chemical dependency. For example, treating alcoholism as a Valium-deficiency is just not okay. (2) The referral agent should be knowledgeable about gay or lesbian persons, realizing that a gay man is not a lesbian and a lesbian not a gay man. Gay society, culture, folk beliefs, oppression and issues are radically different from lesbian society, culture, folk beliefs, oppression and issues. (3) The referral agent should be male-positive if treating gay men, and female-positive for treating lesbians. Likewise, they should be gay-positive if treating gay men and lesbian-positive if treating lesbians. (4) They should have a very open mind regarding spirituality and a working knowledge of AA and other 12-Step programs. Because so many in the gay and lesbian communities live the 12-Step way of life, to not have this basic knowledge would be folly if trying to help such clients.

Like all referrals, social workers should provide the referred client with the opportunity to check in later to report how the referral went for them.

Main Reasons to Treat

Social workers often decide to treat chemically dependent gays or lesbians for a variety of reasons. First, they may have a good knowledge base in the particular issue which the client wants to work on. For example, a gay social worker might have a good background in how to help gay clients treat their internalized homophobia.

Second, there might not be adequate gay or lesbian referral sources. Outside of large and medium-sized cities, for example, there is rarely a specialist in gay or lesbian couples counseling. In this case, social workers who feel confident might decide to counsel gay or lesbian couples, supporting this counseling with solid gay or lesbian readings in the field.

Third, the problem which is presenting itself does not have a gay/lesbian dimension which needs to be considered.

Fourth, clients may resist referrals to gay or lesbian agencies because of severe internalized homophobia, fear of having their sexual orientation becoming known to others, or because they do not like the particular agency in their area to which referral is being considered. In one university town where the primary author was a professor, many young lesbians strongly objected to being referred to the local lesbian group which was noted for its highly militant, anti-male, pro-Marxist orientation. Such clients felt much more comfortable working with mainstream women's counseling groups.

Having discussed some of the considerations in whether to refer or treat, we now turn to possible referral sources.

DISCOVERING RESOURCES FOR GAY AND LESBIAN CLIENTS

Before the death of the old "homophile" movement, and the birth of the gay liberation movement and lesbian feminist movement in 1969, agencies designed to meet the specific needs of gays and lesbians were more or less nonexistent. Today, however, there are many resources available in the United States, especially in the larger cities. In larger cities it is not unusual to find a wide variety of gay and lesbian organizations: social, political, alcoholic recovery, leisure, artistic, scientific, professional, religious, student, faculty, and the like. Generally the larger the city, the more specialized the resources can be. In a large city, for example, one might find a Jewish lesbian non-smoking AA group while in a small college town one would be lucky to find a gay-lesbian mixed AA group.

In less populated parts of America, there are less gay and lesbian resources. However, no matter where one lives in the United States, resources are available even if these must be tapped via telephone, videos, or books.

In this section, we show the reader how to go about finding out what is available in their own communities. Special attention is given to those in rural America.

One, look under "Gay" or "Lesbian" in the *phone book*. You will often be able to find a generalized gay/lesbian group which could be contacted for information about other resources in your area.

Two, make *gay and lesbian friends and colleagues.* They will most likely be your most treasured source of information about resources available in your community.

Three, gay, lesbian, and gay-lesbian groups of AA and other *12-Step groups* (including such groups as Al-Anon for the family and friends of the alcoholic) are found in almost all cities and college towns. Look in the phone book under "AA," "Alcohol Abuse," "Alcohol Treatment," etc. By calling the phone number listed, social workers can often learn where gay or lesbian meetings are held. In some areas of the country, gay and lesbian groups are often called Lambda groups. (The small-case lambda, the 11th letter of the Greek alphabet, stands for "liberation" and is one of the primary symbols of the gay liberation movement.) District meeting schedules of AA, NA (Narcotics Anonymous), CA (Cocaine Anonymous), and other groups provide information about which groups are gay or lesbian, whether or not they are open or closed, and where they meet. They often include phone numbers. Even in rural states there are usually gay and lesbian groups of AA. A list of such groups may be obtained from the International Advisory Council for Homosexual [sic] Men and Women in Alcoholics Anonymous, Inc., by writing for the *World Directory of Gay and Lesbian Meet-*

ings of AA to IAC, PO Box 90, Washington, D.C. 20044. The early 1990s cost of this publication was $5.00.

Human rights organizations such as the American Civil Liberties Union may also be able to provide social workers with information on where to start their search for gay/lesbian resources.

The local *bar association* or *medical society* may be able to refer the social worker to attorneys and physicians noted for their expertise in gay and lesbian issues.

Colleges and universities are almost always a good source to find out what is available in town. In rural areas, colleges and universities are often the chief centers of organized gay or lesbian life. Campus information can direct the social worker to campus gay or lesbian groups. The administration can also tell the caller if there are any gay studies or lesbian studies courses on campus; professors who teach these courses are often a wonderful source of information on where to get help. Be aware, however, that often it is difficult to reach campus groups during the summer months and during Christmas vacation.

AIDS organizations can almost always provide the caller with information on how to contact gay and lesbian groups. Simply look up "AIDS Information," "AIDS Testing," "AIDS Hotlines" and the like in the phone book. All states have an AIDS network structure which can also be used to find out what is available. These sources can also provide information as to support groups for PWAs, groups such as Shanti, AIDS Buddies, and the Chicken Soup Brigade.

Women's groups usually have information about lesbian, and sometimes gay, groups and how to contact them. Looking under "Women," "Women's Organizations," and "NOW" in the phone book is usually sufficient. Because men's liberation, the second part of the gender liberation movement, is just getting started, there are very few resources available to men as men in addressing their issues. Where *men's groups* exist, however, information is usually available about the gay men's community in the area.

Because lesbian society and culture has a strong sports-ethic, many lesbians, when moving to a new area, often find out much of what is available for lesbians in the area by contacting *women's sports groups.*

Computer bulletin boards or *bulletin board systems* often have special bulletin boards for gays and lesbians. One can find the bulletin boards in your area by contacting computer stores, calling up the computer science department at the local college or university, or by looking in the local newspaper's personals or advertisement sections.

Political parties have gay/lesbian caucuses which can also be tapped into for information as to what is available. Republican and Democratic gay/lesbian caucuses can be contacted by calling the local party headquarters.

Local *gay and lesbian newspapers and magazines* are an excellent source of what is available for gays and lesbians in your community. Such papers advertise local gay, lesbian, or gay/lesbian-sensitive physicians, dentists, attorneys, health care facilities, AIDS groups, travel agencies, realtors, social groups, recovery groups and facilities, counseling centers, leisure groups, and the like. Persons can usually get a copy of the local gay/lesbian newspaper by calling the paper, calling local gay/lesbian community centers, asking a gay or lesbian friend to pick one up, looking in gay, lesbian, or alternative bookstores, or from the local gay or lesbian bar.

Bookstores can also be a treasure of resources. Because bibliotherapy, or the use of literature for self-help and personal growth, is so powerful, inexpensive, and everywhere-accessible, helping professionals can always prescribe bibliotherapy to their clients for a variety of issues (Kus, 1989). Because there has been a phenomenal explosion of gay and lesbian literature in recent years, the amount of gay/lesbian resources is staggering. Books on building positive gay or lesbian pride, achieving and maintaining a sober lifestyle, achieving a healthy relationship, meeting spiritual and religious needs, and the like, are all available.

In general bookstores, such books can often be found in these sections: Gay Studies, Lesbian Studies, Men's Studies, Women's Studies, Self-Help, Recovery, and others. In gay and lesbian bookstores, the choices are much greater.

If one is in a very remote part of the country where even a good university bookstore is unavailable, one can call large national gay/lesbian bookstores which will be happy to send the caller an annotated list of books available for purchase by mail. One example is

Lambda Rising Bookstore in Washington, D.C., which can be reached by dialing 1-800-621-6969.

Social workers' own *professional network* can often yield a surprising wealth of information. One can almost always find colleagues who are gay or lesbian themselves or who have intimate knowledge with gay and lesbian persons. The National Association of Social Workers has a National Committee on Lesbian and Gay Issues, 750 First Street, N.E., Suite 700, Washington, D.C. 20002-4241.

Gay and lesbian community centers are generally umbrella organizations providing a number of various services for gays and lesbians. One of the greatest services is to serve as a clearinghouse of information on what is available in the community for gay and lesbian persons. Often these are found in the White Pages or Business Pages of the phone book under the name of the city in which they're found, e.g., "Gotham Gay and Lesbian Community Center."

Crisis hotlines, found in communities of almost any size, usually know where one can turn for gay/lesbian help.

Because many cities have gay/lesbian business organizations, the local *Chamber of Commerce* can be of help in directing the social worker to gay-owned or lesbian-owned businesses which could offer information about what is available to gays and lesbians in the community.

Churches, synagogues, and mosques and other religious centers may be another source of information. Churches which specialize in the needs of gay and lesbian persons, such as the Metropolitan Community Church, are found in almost all large and medium-size cities. Gay/lesbian caucuses are found in all of the major religious denominations, groups such as Dignity for gay/lesbian Roman Catholics, Integrity for Episcopalians, and others. Certain church groups are more likely than others to have information as to what is available for gays/lesbians in the community. Specifically, the Unitarian-Universalist Society and the Unity churches are often on the cutting edge of gay liberation in religious matters and have information on local resources.

Social workers may purchase the *Gayellow Pages* from Lambda Rising or their local bookstore. This book comes in regional and national editions and is a nice reference tool to have in one's library.

Finally, social workers may call NALGAP (National Association of Lesbian and Gay Alcoholism Professionals) for further information, (213) 381-8524.

CONCLUSION

Alcoholism and other forms of chemical dependency can produce problems in all life realms for the addict and his or her loved ones. There are often gay or lesbian "twists" or considerations which must be taken into account for the gay/lesbian recovering client and their loved ones. In this article, we explored some of the gay/lesbian issues which may be present, the issue of whether the social worker should refer or treat, what some resources may be in the social worker's community which may be tapped into for help with gay/lesbian issues, and how to go about finding what is available in the individual social worker's community, even in remote rural areas of America.

REFERENCES

Coleman, E. (Ed.). (1988). *Psychotherapy with homosexual men and women: Integrated identity approaches for clinical practice.* New York: The Haworth Press, Inc.

Crawford, D. (1990). *Easing the ache: Gay men recovering from compulsive behaviors.* New York: Dutton.

Finnegan, D.G. & E.B. McNally. (1987). *Dual identities: Counseling chemically dependent gay men and lesbians.* Center City, MN: Hazelden.

Gay Council on Drinking Behavior. (1981,1982). *The way back: The stories of gay and lesbian alcoholics.* Washington, D.C.: Whitman-Walker Clinic.

Hall, M. (1985). *The lavender couch: A consumer's guide to psychotherapy for lesbians and gay men.* Boston: Alyson.

Kominars, S.B. (1989). *Accepting ourselves: The Twelve-Step journey of recovery from addiction for gay men and lesbians.* San Francisco: Harper & Row, Perennial Library.

Kus, R.J. (1987, July/Aug.). Gay consultations in non-gay treatment settings. *Professional Counselor*, 46-55.

Kus, R.J. (1988). Alcoholism and non-acceptance of gay self: The critical link. *Journal of Homosexuality, 15*(1-2), 25-41.

Kus, R.J. (1989). Bibliotherapy and gay American men of Alcoholics Anonymous. *Journal of Gay and Lesbian Psychotherapy, 1*(2), 73-86.

Kus, R.J. (Ed.). (1990a). *Gay men of Alcoholics Anonymous: First-hand accounts.* North Liberty, IA: WinterStar Press.

Kus, R.J. (Ed.). (1990b). *Keys to caring: Assisting your gay and lesbian clients.* Boston: Alyson.

Kus, R.J. (1991, June). Sobriety, friends, and gay men. *Archives of Psychiatric Nursing, 5*(3), 171-177.

Moses, A.E. & R.O. Hawkins, Jr. (1982). *Counseling lesbian women and gay men: A life-issues approach.* St. Louis: C.V. Mosby Co.

Silverstein, C. (Ed.). (1991). *Gays, lesbians, and their therapists: Studies in psychotherapy.* New York: W.W. Norton.

Weinstein, D.L. (Ed.). (1992). *Lesbians and gay men: Chemical dependency treatment issues.* New York: The Haworth Press, Inc. (Also published as a special issue of the *Journal of Chemical Dependency Treatment*, Vol. 5, No. 1, 1992.)

Woodman, N.J. & H.R. Lenna (1980). *Counseling with gay men and women.* San Francisco: Jossey-Bass.

Ziebold, T.O. & J.O. Mongeon (Eds.) (1982). *Gay and sober: Directions for counseling and therapy.* New York: Harrington Park Press. (Also published as a special issue of the *Journal of Homosexuality,* Vol. 7, No. 4, Summer, 1982.)

Index

Abandonment, fear of, 49
*Accepting Ourselves: The
    Twelve-Step Journey of
    Recovery from Addictions
    for Gay Men and Lesbians*
    (Kominars), 30,94
Acquired immune deficiency
    syndrome (AIDS),
    xxii-xxiii. *See also* Human
    immune deficiency virus
    (HIV) infection; Persons
    with AIDS
  case definition of, 16,17
  deaths due to, 15
  definition of, 16
  effect on chemical dependency
    recovery, 16
  in heterosexuals, 16
  in lesbians, 94
  opportunistic infections of,
    17,22,23
  prophylaxis for, 23
  treatment of, 22-25
  worldwide prevalence of, 15
Addiction. *See also* Alcoholism;
    Chemical dependency;
    Drug abuse
  denial of, 85
  religious, 59,60,65
Addiction professionals, homophobia
    of, 86-87
African-Americans, as Alcoholics
    Anonymous members, 70
AIDS Buddies, 103
AIDS organizations, as gay and
    lesbian resource
    information source, 103
Akron, Bob, xxiv

Al-Anon, 68,86,102
Alcoholics, gay and lesbian
  HIV-positive status of, 94
  internalized homophobia of, 93
Alcoholics Anonymous (AA)
  activity clusters of, 68
  founding of, 67
  gay and lesbian groups in. *See*
    Alcoholics Anonymous,
    special interest groups in
  referrals to, 100
  special interest groups in,
    xxiii-xxiv,3,67-82,86,93-94
  clinical implications of, 80
  definition of, 68,69
  historical background of, 70
  homonegativity and, 71
  how to locate, 102-103
  limitations of, 76-78
  need for, 70-72
  positive aspects of, 72-76
  in rural areas, 79-80
  sponsorship policy of, 77
  types of, 69-70
  spirituality component of, 68,
    73-74,75,94
  Third Tradition of, 68,70
  "working through the program"
    concept of, 68,72
Alcoholics Anonymous Grapevine,
    xxiv
Alcoholics Anonymous World
    Services, 79
Alcoholism
  as AIDS risk factor, xxiii
  denial of, 84,85
  incidence studies of, 2,5-14
  Fifield study, 6,9

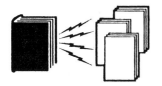

Haworth
DOCUMENT DELIVERY
SERVICE

This new service provides a single-article order form for any article from a Haworth journal.

- *Time Saving:* No running around from library to library to find a specific article.
- *Cost Effective:* All costs are kept down to a minimum.
- *Fast Delivery:* Choose from several options, including same-day FAX.
- *No Copyright Hassles:* You will be supplied by the original publisher.
- *Easy Payment:* Choose from several easy payment methods.

Open Accounts Welcome for ...
- **Library Interlibrary Loan Departments**
- **Library Network/Consortia Wishing to Provide Single-Article Services**
- **Indexing/Abstracting Services with Single Article Provision Services**
- **Document Provision Brokers and Freelance Information Service Providers**

MAIL or *FAX* THIS ENTIRE ORDER FORM TO:

Attn: **Marianne Arnold**
Haworth Document Delivery Service
The Haworth Press, Inc.
10 Alice Street
Binghamton, NY 13904-1580

or **FAX:** (607) 722-1424
or **CALL:** 1-800-3-HAWORTH
(1-800-342-9678; 9am-5pm EST)

PLEASE SEND ME PHOTOCOPIES OF THE FOLLOWING SINGLE ARTICLES:

1) Journal Title: _____
   Vol/Issue/Year:_____Starting & Ending Pages:_____
   Article Title:_____
_____

2) Journal Title: _____
   Vol/Issue/Year:_____Starting & Ending Pages:_____
   Article Title:_____
_____

3) Journal Title: _____
   Vol/Issue/Year:_____Starting & Ending Pages:_____
   Article Title:_____
_____

4) Journal Title: _____
   Vol/Issue/Year:_____Starting & Ending Pages:_____
   Article Title:_____
_____

(See other side for Costs and Payment Information)

COSTS: Please figure your cost to order quality copies of an article.

1. Set-up charge per article: $8.00
   ($8.00 × number of separate articles)   _____

2. Photocopying charge for each article:

   1-10 pages: $1.00   _____

   11-19 pages: $3.00   _____

   20-29 pages: $5.00   _____

   30+ pages: $2.00/10 pages   _____

3. Flexicover (optional): $2.00/article   _____

4. Postage & Handling: US: $1.00 for the first article/

   $.50 each additional article   _____

   Federal Express: $25.00   _____

   Outside US: $2.00 for first article/

   $.50 each additional article_____

5. Same-day FAX service: $.35 per page   _____

GRAND TOTAL: _____

METHOD OF PAYMENT: (please check one)

❑ Check enclosed   ❑ Please ship and bill. PO # _____
                      (sorry we can ship and bill to bookstores only! All others must pre-pay)

❑ Charge to my credit card: ❑ Visa;   ❑ MasterCard; ❑ American Express;

Account Number: _____ Expiration date:_____

Signature: ✗_____ Name: _____

Institution: _____ Address: _____

City: _____ State:_____ Zip:_____

Phone Number: _____ FAX Number: _____

MAIL or *FAX* THIS ENTIRE ORDER FORM TO:

Attn: **Marianne Arnold**
Haworth Document Delivery Service
The Haworth Press, Inc.
10 Alice Street
Binghamton, NY 13904-1580

or **FAX:** (607) 722-1424
or **CALL:** 1-800-3-HAWORTH
(1-800-342-9678; 9am-5pm EST)